DRESSAGE
IN THE
FRENCH TRADITION

Dom Diogo de Bragança

XENOPHON PRESS

DRESSAGE
IN THE
FRENCH TRADITION

DOM DIOGO DE BRAGANÇA

Translated from Portuguese by René Bacharach

Translated from French by Michael L. M. Fletcher

Copyright © 2011 Xenophon Press LLC

All rights reserved

From

Original edition:

L'Équitation de tradition Française

© Éditions Belin - Paris, 2005

Title: *DRESSAGE IN THE FRENCH TRADITION*

by Dom Diogo de Bragança

Copyright © 2011 by Xenophon Press LLC

Translated by Michael L. M. Fletcher

Edited by Richard and Frances Williams

All rights reserved. No part of this work may be reproduced or transmitted in any form or by any means, electronic or mechanical, including photocopying, or by any information storage or retrieval system except by a written permission from the publisher.

Published by Xenophon Press LLC

7518 Bayside Road, Franktown, Virginia 23354-2106, U.S.A.

ISBN ISBN-10 0933316216

ISBN-13 9780933316218

e-Book ISBN: 9780933316607

Original French Edition: *L'Equitation de Tradition Français*

ISBN: 978701135625

Copyright Editions Belin Paris 2005

Cover Photograph: Rijo, ridden by Dom Diogo de Bragança

This work on dressage
is dedicated to Master *Écuyer* Nuno Oliveira,
in testimony of friendship, admiration,
and gratitude of his student.

-Dom Diogo de Bragança

Rijo, ridden by Dom Diogo de Bragança

TABLE OF CONTENTS

FOREWORD TO THE ENGLISH EDITION by Miguel Tavora vii

ENGLISH PUBLISHER'S DEDICATION vii

INTRODUCTION TO THE ENGLISH EDITION viii

PREFACE TO CURRENT EDITION by Dom Diogo de Bragança ,,,,,,..2

PREFACE TO ORIGINAL EDITION by René Bacharach 4

PART ONE: THE SCIENCE AND ART OF EQUITATION 7

Introduction 7

CHAPTER 1: CHARACTERISTICS OF ACADEMIC EQUITATION: THE *RASSEMBLER* 9

Origins of the *Rassembler* 10

The *Rassembler* and its Requirements 11

The *Ramener* 18

The Engagement of the Hindquarters 22

Flexibility 24

Lightness 27

CHAPTER 2: LIMITS OF THE *RASSEMBLER* 31

Limits of the *Ramener* 31

Limits of Engagement of the Hindquarters 33

Limits of Flexibility 38

Limits of Lightness 39

PART TWO: SYSTEMS OF HORSEMANSHIP 43

Introduction 43

CHAPTER 1: THE OLD SCHOOL 45

Gineta, *Estradiota*, and *Brida* 45

Origins and Development 48

Organization 55

The Goal 59

The Method 60

La Guérinière's Progression 61

The Trot as the Basic Gait of Dressage 64

General Actions 64

The Old School *Rassembler* 67

La Guérinière's "Square" 68

The Old School Airs 68

The Old School of Portugal 71

Luz de l'Arte Liberal e Nobre de Cavalaria 72

The Art of Marialva 74

Examination of Old School Equitation 75

CHAPTER 2: BAUCHER'S SYSTEM 79

Antecedents 79

Baucherism and Romanticism 81

Baucherism and the Circus 83

Baucher's Teaching Methods, First Manner 86

Baucher's Teaching Methods, Second Manner 92

Examination of Baucher's Methods 98

Walk, the Gait at the Base of Dressage 100

The Position of the Horse's Head at the Beginning of Dressage 100

Flexions 105

Rassembler at the Halt in the First Manner 106

"Hand without Legs, Legs without Hand"...107

Diagonal Aids and Lateral Aids 109

Placing the Horse in Position 111

The Spurs... 113

General Actions and Partial Actions 114

Resistances of Weight and Force... 115

General and Partial Actions used Simultaneously 116

Baucher's Two Manners 116

Gineta, Baucher, and Bullfighting 118

PART THREE: CURRENT OVERVIEW OF ACADEMIC HORSEMANSHIP 121

Introduction 121

CHAPTER 1: ACADEMIC HORSEMANSHIP IN F. E. I. PROGRAMS 125

The Preference Given to Horses with Naturally Ample Gaits 126

Same Coefficient for Exercises of Different Difficulty 128

Greater Importance Given to the Precision of an Exercise to the

Detriment of its Beauty 129

Exhibitions and Competitions 137

Greater Importance of Germanic Criteria in International Juries 137

The Concept of Lightness 138

Lightness and Supportive Contact (*appui*) 141

The Horse "On the Hand" and the Horse "Behind the Hand"...............146

Holding the Reins 151

Judging Criteria 152

CHAPTER 2: CONTEMPORARY ACADEMIC HORSEMANSHIP IN PORTUGAL 155

Bullfighting Horsemanship and its Merit in Relation to Dressage 156

The Horse Fair at Golegã 168

Horsemanship methods from the valley of the Tejo 173

The Airs Practiced in Horsemanship from the valley of the Tejo 174

CHAPTER 3: CRITIQUE OF THE BAUCHERIST CONCEPT OF ACADEMIC HORSEMANSHIP 177

The Principles Apply to Every Horse 177

Methods Are Personal to Each *Écuyer* 184

A Note on Exercises and Airs 187

The Goal of Dressage is Unique 190

BIBLIOGRAPHY 191

CREDITS 195

XENOPHON PRESS LIBRARY 197

FOREWORD TO THE ENGLISH EDITION

Once more Michael Fletcher presents us with a careful translation of a book. It is with great pleasure that I write this foreword. Diogo is a great friend of mine and a fellow student of Nuno Oliveira. Diogo makes a deep study of the methods of the Old School and those of Baucher. All students interested in studying the history of dressage must understand the influence of the former and the latter on modern dressage. At last, English speaking people have the opportunity to study a clear and accurate summary.

Michael did a very accurate translation without distorting the sense of what the author intended to express; this is rare in the translation of equestrian books. Also, as with previous books, Michael was careful and clear in explaining the meaning of French words that don't have direct translation into English.

Thank you, Michael for all of your hard work.

Major Miguel Tavora (Portuguese Cavalry Retired)

ENGLISH PUBLISHER'S DEDICATION

Xenophon Press and the English readership owe a special debt of gratitude to Michael L. M. Fletcher who passionately and tirelessly worked on the English translation of this great work. He also brought this important book to our attention for publication. It is with joy that we are able to see Michael's work come to fruition and with great sadness that we realize Michael did not see this work in print. He was an avid scholar, passionate about translating important French equestrian works.

In this pivotal book, Dom Diogo de Bragança brings into new perspective the evolution and history of French dressage which need not have national boundaries. His love and compassion for the horse come through on every page. Bragança illuminates how to ride our horses with the ultimate reward for both horse and rider. Harmony and lightness are clearly and passionately explained, shown through rich images and historical research and references. This book represents a turning point in understanding and illumination on the Art of Riding.

Richard F. Williams, Xenophon Press

INTRODUCTION TO THE ENGLISH EDITION

Since General Decarpentry's *Academic Equitation* was first published in 1949, Dom Diogo de Bragança's masterpiece, *Dressage in the French Tradition* is *the* most important book written on the subject of French dressage during the past half-century. This complex and fascinating subject has piqued the curiosity of English-speaking riders in recent years. A clear overview of the various schools of thought had been missing until now. When it was first published in French, *Dressage in the French Tradition* by Diogo de Bragança was a major milestone for passionate French speaking dressage riders searching for a better sense of their hallowed antecedents' works. Now it can finally be read in English.

Bragança's masterpiece helps us grasp the evolution of the theory of horse training. The matching of goals with the right methods creates the solutions we need. It is the practical link between the dream of equestrian artistry and the reality of resolving problems presented to us by less than perfect horses.

The history of horsemanship has been a continuum in which every innovation stemmed from a previous situation. Iberian horses always displayed a talent for collection. The Iberian breeds were refined through centuries of fighting with the Romans and later the Moorish invaders on the Peninsula. The Italians of the Renaissance, full of envy for the horses of their friendly Spanish occupants, conceptualized collection for the training of "regular" horses and gave dressage all of its terminology which was then translated into the French terms that we use today (piaffe, passage, levade, courbette, etc.) The young French aristocrats of the time who studied in Italy brought dressage back to their country and made it one of the most important royal courtly pursuits. French *écuyers* perfected dressage through three and a half centuries of enthusiastic creativity devoted both to artistic and military horsemanship.

During and after the French Revolution, the French masters taught abroad, making La Guérinière's *École de Cavalerie* (*The School of Horsemanship, Part II,* Xenophon Press 1992) the "Bible" of Vienna, Berlin and Hannover, adapted through the filter of Germanic temperament. Later, the German speaking world resisted the influence of Baucher's revolutionary concepts, more for nationalistic reasons than objective examination. And they remained loyal to La Guérinière.

Baucher dealt with both hot blooded horses (Thoroughbreds or derivatives) as well as some draught-types. Neither type was gifted at the High School movements that the public had come to expect from the presentations of the *Écuyers* of the Royal School of Versailles on talented Iberian horses. By inventing a new approach to the progression of training, Baucher paved the way for all riders faced with horses that are less than perfect in their conformation, balance and energy.

The central ideas of French dressage so masterfully explained by Bragança show the differences between the *"general actions"* used by the classical masters: good rider position, shoulder-in, half-passes, halts and half-halts, transitions and gait variations, and the *"partial actions"*: flexions, hands without legs, legs without hands, pirouettes and reversed pirouettes, proposed by Baucher and his followers. The author shows with great clarity which actions suit which type of horse at different stages of training. He analyzes the limits of each concept according to conformation and temperament. Master Nuno Oliveira, the teacher of Dom Diogo, gave us a new model that integrated the approaches of La Guérinière and Baucher in a very pragmatic methodology. Oliveira's dressage synthesis suited many types and allowed him to train an amazing number of beautifully finished horses. Bragança himself trained many horses and made it his goal to explore the limits of the methods by buying very different 'project' horses. His presentation of the methods of the past is based on his very real experience in the present.

What is the relevance of the French dressage tradition today? In recent decades, Jean-Claude Racinet, Michel Henriquet, Nuno Oliveira and others have explained the French tradition in their writings, their teaching and their practices. Bragança originally published this seminal book in 1975, bringing us a lucid overview of the methods of the past with all their technical implications for every type of horse.

Instead of being simply a repository of history, a curiosity for riders romantically interested in past traditions, *Dressage in the French Tradition* is the blueprint needed to improve the performance of all horses and riders, gifted or not. Fritz Stahlecker, a German master of in-hand work, found his inspiration in the French School and said: "The French are the real inventors of dressage." His work is based on early development of collection: piaffe, pirouettes, and Spanish walk. Yet his results in big dressage competition show the validity of this approach, well-explained by Bragança. An educated form of dressage inspired by the French masters can have a successful application in modern competition.

Dom Diogo wrote commentary on the judging criteria of dressage competition in 1959. His foresight proved correct. He pointed out many of the problems that have since been addressed by the FEI, with the exception of lightness. The combination of the lightness of the aids and the amplitude of the gaits is the hallmark of High School Dressage. Though lofty, it is the only goal worth pursuing if we care for the happiness of the horse, the true beauty of the dressage spectacle, and our own development as 'centaurs'.

It is ironic that a rider from Portugal should be the one telling us about *Dressage in the French Tradition*. His country is a small but very ancient nation that has had a relationship with France for centuries, a devotion to horses, and a passion for their training bridging all classes of society. Different periods of history of Iberian horsemanship are brilliantly represented in Portugal by riders of talent and have been absorbed by a population whose original name, Lusitania, issued from a Greek word that means "the land of the riders."

Dressage and horsemanship are in Dom Diogo's blood. He descends from ten kings of Portugal back to Dom Afonso the Conqueror who was himself a direct descendant of the French kings. Dom Afonso defeated the Moors and established Portugal as the oldest country of Europe. His ancestor, Dom Duarte (in 1434) produced the most ancient treatise on horsemanship since Xenophon: *The Art of Riding in Every Saddle,* Chivalry Bookshelf 2005). Dom Diogo also descends from five *Estribeiro-Mor,* Royal Masters of the Horse through the Marquis of Marialva, the most famous *écuyer* in Portuguese history, whose title he carries to this day. Several of his family members were practitioners of academic dressage while others were bullfighters. He was an eclectic student, earning a law degree and studying music composition at the Lisbon Conservatory. Dom Diogo began studying horsemanship at a very young age at the School of Antonio Correia in Lisbon and continued with Master Nuno Oliveira, with whom he studied for 8 years.

I quote here Andre Montheillet from *The Masters of the Equestrian Literature* (Odege, 1977, pg 60): "Because (as a young man) Dom Diogo did not have the means to buy good horses -- the ones we say are 'born trained'-- he had to train some that had only very mediocre qualities, or worse, those which had been ruined by less than expert hands. Yet he never abandoned the light actions that belonged to his equestrian ethic. He became an *écuyer*, gifted not only with a great tact, both natural and acquired, but also with a degree of virtuosity that permitted him to obtain from his horses a high level of impulsion, mobility and brilliance. Dom Diogo, along with his daily practice, methodical and patient, spent time observing and reflecting, as well as reading the works of the *écuyers* of the past, the good ones and the less good ones. His critical mind, always alert, had helped him to write down a few important concepts in his notebooks. His friend René Bacharach, on holiday at Torre-Bela, read them. There, he found the most complete and correct analysis ever made of the different historical equestrian methods. Dom Diogo appeared to be the *premier comparateur* of the various systems of horsemanship. René Bacharach translated this original work and it was published in 1975 under the title *Equitation de Tradition Française* (*Dressage in the French Tradition,* Xenophon Press 2011).

Montheillet, who researched the life and works of one hundred and sixty of the most important writers of equestrian history, placed *Dressage in the French Tradition* on the level of the works of La Guérinière, Baucher, L'Hotte, Beudant, Decarpentry and Podhajsky.

In spite of his significant ancestry and many personal accomplishments, Dom Diogo is a humble and humorous man who spent, as he says "a lot of time reading books he did not agree with." Armed with Dom Diogo's encompassing vision and luminous explanations, we and our horses are all better off.

I first saw Dom Diogo ride in 1973 at the equestrian gala organized at the formerly royal stud farm in Alter do Chao for the purpose of saving the Alter Real breed from its chronic lack of funding. I was living in Alter then, studying and working as an assistant trainer. On the days preceding the gala, I observed the work of the famous *écuyers* who came to support this great cause. Dom Diogo was riding a tall gray horse called Intrepido, wearing a faded green *casaca* that had belonged to one of his royal ancestors. A *casaca* is a coat that is part of the traditional XVIII century costume worn by bullfighters and *écuyers*. A good friend whispered to me that Dom Diogo was a "Baucherist" and did not practice shoulder-in, unlike other students of master Oliveira.

His skill and this fact ignited my curiosity about the man. I travelled to see him at Torrebella, the hunting farm he had inherited from his royal family. I watched him ride one of his fabulously well-trained horses then I listened to him speak eloquently about dressage.

A few years later, I travelled to Paris to support the nascent Portuguese School of Equestrian Art. My teacher Dom Jose d'Athayde was the first head rider at that time. My dear friends, Francisco Cancella d'Abreu and Joao Filipe Graciosa were the founding riders along with Joao Trigueiros d'Aragao. One can see many pictures of Trigueiros d'Aragao in *Dressage in the French Tradition*. Dom Diogo travelled to Paris with the group and I had more conversations with him then. He wore custom shoes with old-fashioned white spats. He had mistakenly packed a brown left shoe and a black right shoe, which he wore all week long without an ounce of self-consciousness. Our leisurely walk along the Seine on the way to René Bacharach's apartment cemented my fascination for one of the great equestrian minds of our time.

Dressage in the French Tradition is very personal to me because I had the good fortune to refine my riding on some of the magnificently trained horses shown in its pages: Violaceo, Formoso and Jiorno. I also observed Hioral and Ansioso during their daily training. Having studied many of these riders, I can vouch unequivocally that they could actually demonstrate the ideals of lightness in motion and brilliance laced with relaxation. They proved that classical dressage in the French tradition is the true poetry of horsemanship.

Jean Philippe Giacomini

"I have spent much of my time reading books
with which I did not agree."
-Dom Diogo de Bragança

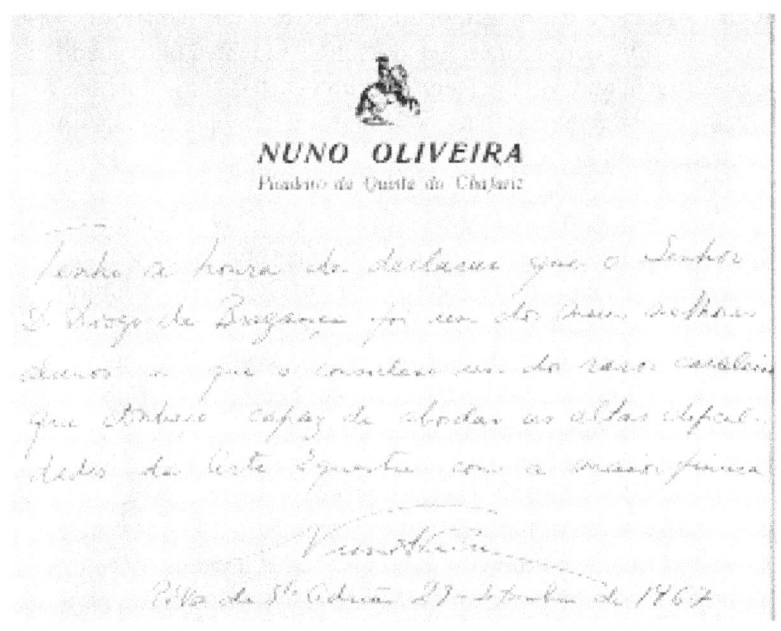

"I have the honor to declare that Mr. D. Diogo de Bragança has been one of my best students and that I consider him as one of the rare riders that I know to be capable of taking on the highest difficulties of Equestrian Art with the greatest finesse."
-Nuno Oliveira
Povoa de Santo Adriào, 29 September 1967

PREFACE TO THE CURRENT EDITION

Thirty years have passed since René Bacharach first read this work which he translated, faithful to the Portuguese text, for publication in 1975. It is with great emotion that I remember this friend, now departed, such a great loss to the equestrian culture of the French tradition.

It was over the course of this period that the great master Nuno Oliveira also passed. He was an emblematic rider and *écuyer* of worldwide renown, to whom France found itself so indebted once Jean Persin, René Bacharach, and Michel Henriquet met each other in Lisbon, where they finally found a master that had been formed by horsemanship in the French tradition in Portugal!

Watching him ride Lusitano horses, which at that time, they did not know as well as horses of a variety of other breeds, they discovered an *écuyer* who reconciled the doctrines of the Old School with those of Baucher. Such a fusion of equestrian doctrines had already been accomplished by certain *écuyer*s during the second half of the XIX Century and up until the Second World War, but without a doubt had lacked a hallmark representative since then.

Nuno Oliveira had acquired a profound theoretical knowledge from assiduous study of the writings of the great masters. But on a horse, it was his tact that inspired his French visitors. "One must have tact in the hands, in the legs, and above all in the head," he wrote in the *Vida Rural* review. This reflection demonstrated how much he judged it necessary to adapt acquired knowledge to each horse. "Put into practice, theory becomes something else!" The riders of our day imagined with difficulty the conformation weaknesses and faults in horses that our generation had to put in balance, each one requiring his own tact, in order to function normally or to succeed at "such and such" a school air.

With the death of the great bullfighting rider, João Nuncio, we have also lost an exceptional artist, who in the arena presented French equestrian art applied to combat with a bull.

These past thirty years have meanwhile brought very positive elements, first among them a remarkable effort of selection in the raising of the Lusitano that has led to its substantial improvement and to its appreciation in France, Belgium, Germany, Spain, Mexico, and particularly in Brazil, where excellent examples are bred.

The creation of the Portuguese School of Equestrian Art in 1979, thanks to the devotion and competence of Dr. Guilherme Borba and a special group of *écuyers*, has allowed numerous riders to receive an education and practice the most beautiful form of horsemanship at the highest standard.

The enthusiastic development of tests of working equitation and Tauromachic Horsemanship (used in bullfighting) has renewed interest in many young people for practical horsemanship that, in conferring a more solid base for training will always be an indispensable preparation for artistic dressage. Numerous tests of this sort are organized nowadays in various countries, and this intense activity has allowed Portuguese riders to win World Championships in working equitation.

The organization of the equestrian fair in Golegã and of the Lusitano Horse Festival in Lisbon have made great progress. Prize money and the quality of the horses always draw as many fans worldwide as those from Portugal.

FEI dressage tests have equally seen notable progress, not only in the evolution of criteria for classification used by judges, but also in the diversification of breeds presented, and in the introduction of new tests, notably the freestyle tests to music that are of more artistic quality.

The new edition of this work is augmented with some notes on the way to ride *a la Gineta, Estardiota e Brida*, and on the relationship between Baucher's First Manner and riding *a la Gineta*.

It has been my hope to gather together elements for my readers that, although presented from a Portuguese viewpoint, have as their goal to enrich and augment the inexhaustible patrimony that is the French Equestrian Tradition.

Lisbon, 8 May 2003

Dom Diogo de Bragança

PREFACE TO THE ORIGINAL EDITION

Dom Diogo de Bragança defines himself as a permanent and enthusiastic student of equestrian art. In his country, Portugal, there is not only a set of elite riders that train their horses with a remarkable delicacy as much with the leg as with the hand, but also a certain number of emulators who ride visibly with the same care.

A French friend of the author once expressed his amazement at the surprising deftness of Portuguese horsemanship. He received this response: "But it is French dressage."

The ideal of traditional French dressage is to get to the descent of the hand and the leg. "It is lightness that gives at the same time to learned horsemanship, to high school dressage, its veritable cachet, and to the *écuyer* who practices it, the true character of his talent." General L'Hotte.

And yet lightness is not just a lost art, it has fallen into a veritable discredit internationally. One can consider this very regrettable and unjustified. For all that, to ride one's horse in lightness is still, today, in Portugal, the manner of good riders. When bullfighting on horseback, for which they have kept their costumes of the XVIII Century, they are like living engravings of a form of French dressage in which we see an example for ourselves. Lightness is a vital necessity in the bullfighting arena. It has been maintained there by means inherited from the great French *écuyers*. Without it, bullfighting riders of quality would not get from their horses the extreme mobility of the *rassembler*[1] that is indispensable when confronting the bull. It is the equestrian "moment of truth." This combat therefore remains the indirect cause of the survival of authentic classical dressage.

In *Dressage in the French Tradition*, Dom Diogo de Bragança examines the requirements of what Dupaty de Clam calls, "The Science and Art of Dressage." He notes the results obtained in dressage by the old methods with Portuguese horses who are the descendants of those that adorn the old books. He goes on to take further note of the results obtained with these same horses on the one hand, and with hot-blooded horses (thoroughbreds and derivatives) on the other hand, thanks to the discoveries of Baucher and thanks to the dressage of those who, according to General Decarpentry's lucid remark, worked "from Baucherism without knowing it."

---

1 Collection

Bragança analyzes the concepts and methods of French horsemanship, and admirably makes us understand their similarities and differences.

In our time when Baucherism, after having been very much attacked and vilified, is no longer in fashion, the author can surprise us by the profession of a very Baucherist faith; he subtly explains himself in making clear that one must not forget that Baucher was constantly varying his techniques, and that to be a Baucherist is to be above all a perpetual researcher.

While *Dressage in the French Tradition* is not an actual method, does not contain lessons, nor advice, the principles of two great systems of horsemanship are discussed with such clarity that the book could be very beneficial to all riders who care to re-examine all that they have learned from teachers, from horses and from specialized books; in effect, from all that is necessary for an in depth equestrian education. Alois Podhajsky said: "Knowledge must always precede action." Apart from this knowledge, one must not lose the view that great results are only attained with years of methodical and patient work, perseverance and profound study, with the rider alert to all occasions to refine his equestrian tact in order to come to the practice of true art.

The author clarifies perfectly the *raisons d'être* of dressage, of what one could call basic horsemanship, which has its role in every equestrian discipline. Diogo de Bragança offers us his final reflection in the form of an "Overview of Current School Horsemanship." In it he deplores the "Preponderance Given to the Precision of an Exercise to the Detriment of Its Beauty." In enunciating this observation that, despite its seeming impertinence, is on the contrary very pertinent, he makes us reflect on what Commandant Licart loved to say, "The truth is not always a good thing to say, but it is always the good thing to hear."

René Bacharach (1903 – 1991)

Translator of the Original French Edition

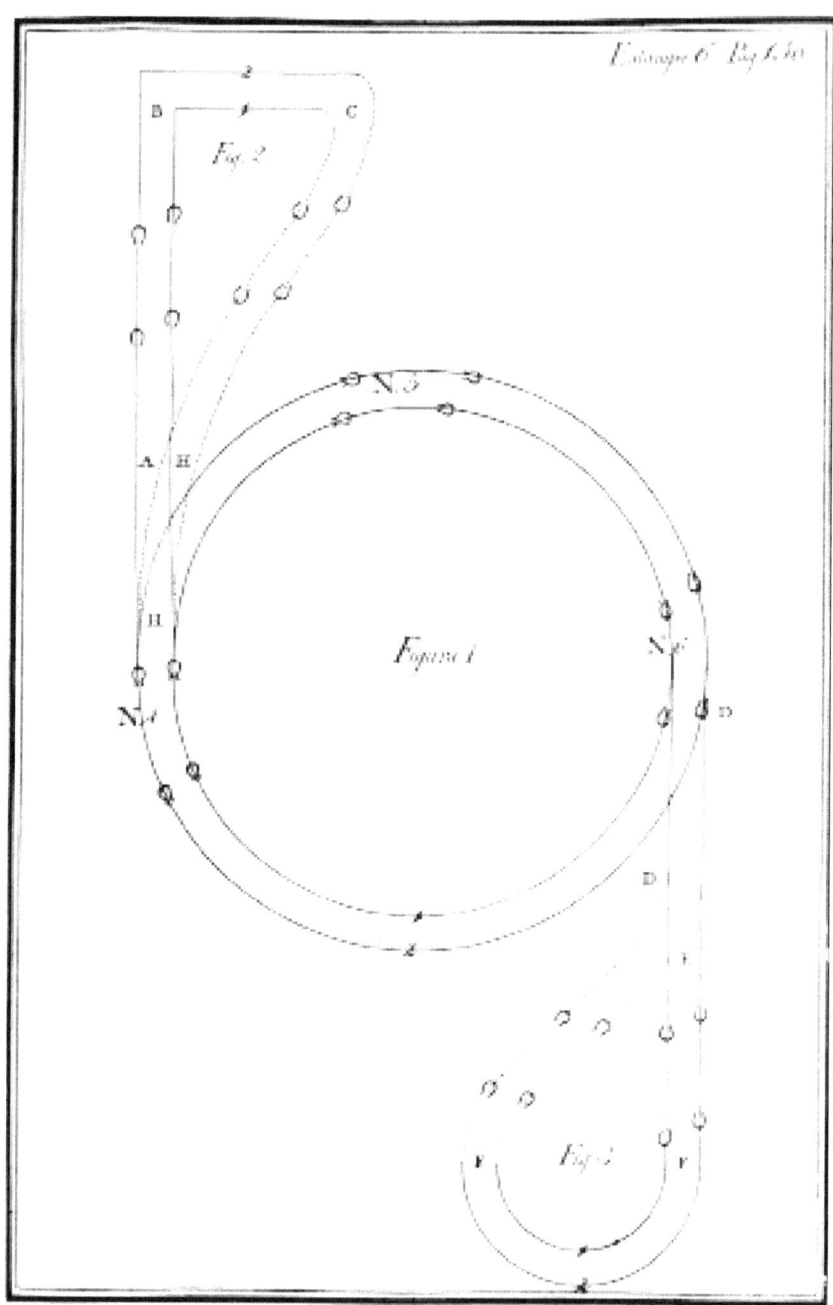

Work on circles and half-circles.

PART ONE

THE SCIENCE AND ART OF EQUITATION

Dupaty de Clam (1744 – 1782), a former musketeer, educated enough at the age of twenty-five to become a member of the Academy of Sciences, Letters, and Arts of Bordeaux, founded by Montesquieu, brought out, at the age of thirty-two in 1776, a reasoned and methodical study entitled *La Science & l'Art de l'Équitation* (The Science and Art of Equitation), a milestone in equestrian literature. With the greatest modesty, he "justified" this important book by saying that he had sensed "the utility, and even the necessity, to bring together the theoretical study and the exercise of riding the horse." (p. 8.) He wished "that students would have preliminary theoretical knowledge before arriving at the *manège*[2]." (pp. 20, 21) His precocious maturity has left us a brilliant masterwork. At least, one can say that his exposé of horsemanship is embellished and endlessly clarified by observation due to the most delicate practice. It is in homage to such a great work that we have borrowed his title for the following study of the *rassembler* and its requirements.

---

2 School, arena, usually indoors

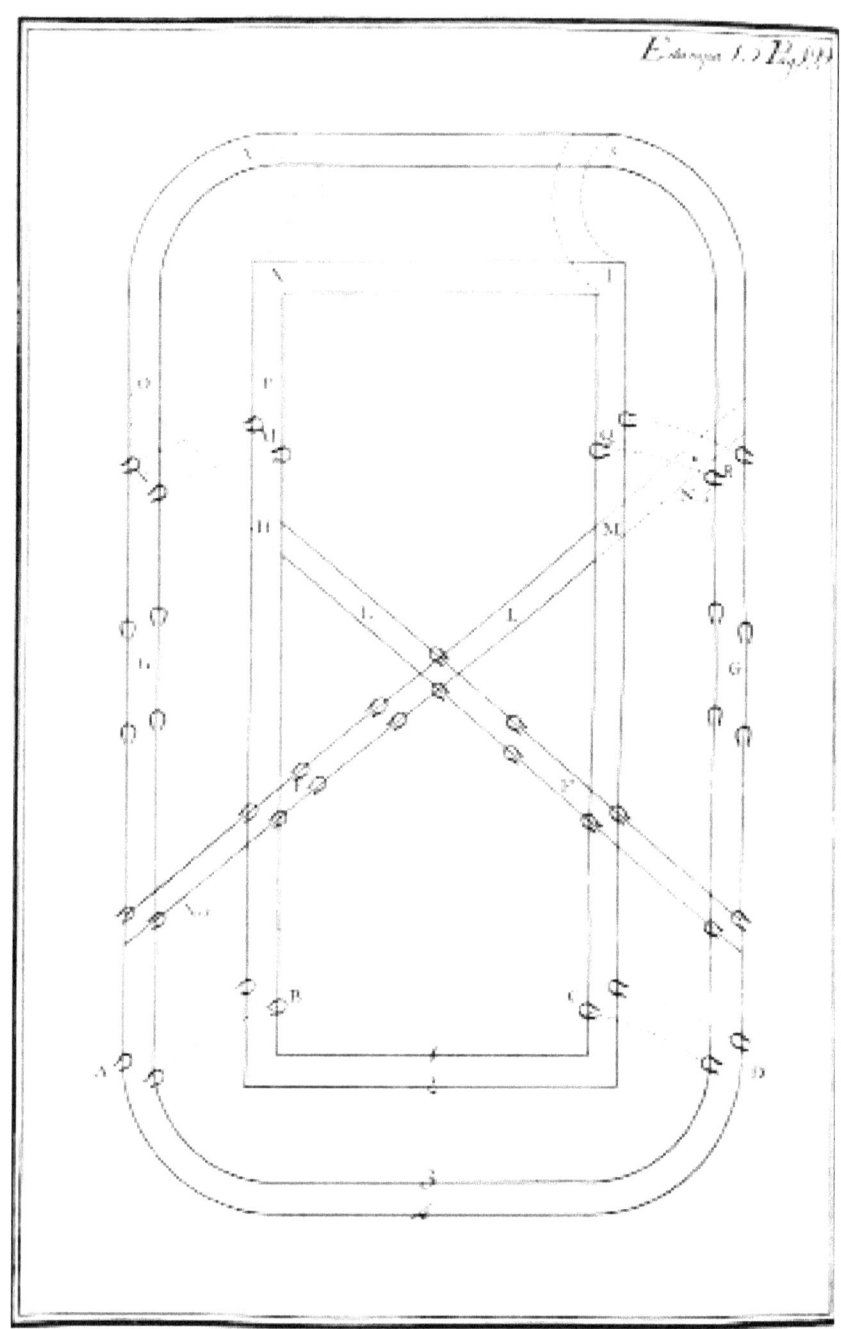

Shoulder-in and change of hand.

CHAPTER 1

CHARACTERISTICS OF ACADEMIC EQUITATION:

THE *RASSEMBLER*

In beginning the study of what we call Academic Dressage, we are presented with two specific ideas, that of the *rassembler* and that of lightness. We will consider the second as an easy means for the rider to apply the aids, and for the horse to respond, and the first as a balance or equilibrium on a short (collected) base of support (the horse's feet placed close together).

We prefer the concept of the *rassembler* as *the characteristic* of School Horsemanship, which does not mean that we discount the value of lightness, but that we reckon that the idea of collection as required by High School, or the conjunction of forces necessary to its practice, finds its best expression in the *rassembler*, which is the harmonization of the means necessary for the execution of natural gaits, or those that are derived from them, on a short base of support.

Lightness is conceived as a requirement of the *rassembler*, among other things, and not as a quality that by itself indicates that a horse is schooled in an academic fashion.

Even though there have been passionate discussions and various interpretations of the real value of lightness, the great majority of *écuyers* consider the *rassembler* absolutely indispensable to true High School, and consequently, when referring to any method, they have always defined the form of the *rassembler* by the interpretations of the great equestrian schools. Thus one speaks of the "sitting *rassembler*" on the haunches in the Old School, of the horizontal *rassembler* in Baucher's First Manner, or of the *rassembler* without the concentration of forces in Baucher's Second Manner.

It appears to me that Pellier fils (Jr.) had a reason when he wrote "High School being only the extension and perfected practice of the principles that serve as the base of dressage in general. We will call it exactly: *équitation rassemblée* (dressage in the *rassembler*)." (J. Pellier fils, *L'Équitation practique*, 3ᵉ éd. 1875, p. 133.)

ORIGINS OF THE *RASSEMBLER*

The *rassembler* of academic dressage was first seen in the Iberian horse.

After the invasion of the Iberian Peninsula by the Arabs in the VIII Century, the invaders were mercilessly counter-attacked and harassed by the Christian Celt-Iberians for seven-hundred years until they were permanently driven out after the capture of Grenada by the Catholic Kings in 1492.

Thanks to their horses, whose qualities, outside of natural selection over millennia, never ceased to improve with war, the adversaries of the Moors had arrived at "an excellence in combat on horseback, never attained until then, and never surpassed since." (Ruy d'Andrade, *Boletim pecuario*, Lisbon, Jan. 1943.)

The horses of the peninsula had taken on a posture so collected that halts, rein-backs, turns, steps to the side, and sudden departs were performed easily. They put at the disposal of their riders an extraordinary weapon: mobility in every direction.

Ferdinand the Catholic was a pretender to the Kingdom of Naples, as was the King of France Charles VIII. The battle turned to the advantage of the Spaniards. It was then that the Italians of the Renaissance discovered the horses from the Iberian Peninsula. Not having been able to obtain from their mounts what they had seen done with the greatest facility by the Spaniards, they were driven to invent training rules permitting them to bring their horses to the degree of collection observed in the peninsular horses, who in that collected equilibrium disposed themselves with the greatest of ease. Therefore it was the horses of Iberian breeding that served as models for the Italians, thus enabling the discovery of the different airs and school jumps. To learn a passage or a pesade would never have come up in the mind of a rider unless he had seen or felt a horse execute them. It was the *écuyer's* challenge to discover a method conducive to preparing horses which, by their constitution or temperament, would be less apt to the execution of the airs.

Thus was born the science of horsemanship.

Through methodical and deep study of cause and effect, its essential function was to find the progressions of mental and physical gymnastics that allow non-peninsular horses to carry themselves under their riders with impulsion and dexterity comparable to that deployed by Iberian horses.

Horses worth educating to become good "School" horses, or as said today according to a questionable but prevalent label, good "dressage" horses, must present, outside of the favorable qualities of conformation and character, the primordial quality that is made up of energy, natural impulsion, and sensitivity, and that which we call: blood.

Perhaps this opinion will not be shared by those who have a concept of contemporary horsemanship as "dressage", totally different from that which the peninsular horses have shown us.

If I take the opinion that the blood horse is the best for School dressage, I think that I must practice with such a horse exactly what I really understand as horsemanship, in all that it comprises in study, modification of the balance, tact, and method. Academic dressage must be used to achieve with the horse a *rassembler* that would be as close as possible to that of the peninsular horse. If an Iberian horse naturally possesses the *rassembler* that serves as our example, it is evident that the dressage we would practice with him will present much less difficulty. There will not be as much preparation required to bring the horse into desired balance. This balance already exists; what is simply required is to develop it. With a blood horse, if he is not a peninsular horse, the *écuyer* must prepare the *rassembler*. With the peninsular horse, he must not undermine the *rassembler* that the horse is disposed to give him. With the first, there is a real horsemanship problem that the rider must solve; with the second, there is a natural balance that the rider must respect.

THE *RASSEMBLER* AND ITS REQUIREMENTS

Academic dressage is characterized by a superior use of the horse, during which he must work in balance on a short base of support. I am not excluding the possibility of a transition to a more extended (or horizontal) balance. But when the *écuyer* practices this variation, the return to a collected balance must be done without difficulty, and the horse must remain in that collected balance as long as his rider requires it.

We consider the *rassembler* the characteristic of High School. However, it is not a position that the horse does not come out of. Instead, the horse achieves a balance (in the *rassembler*) into which he comes, then leaves, and ultimately returns.

Many authors consider the *rassembler* to be an air, or a simple movement, that the horse executes in place with diagonal steps, more or less precipitated, that could be the prelude to piaffe. At the beginning, Baucher accepted this concept bringing the fore and hind legs of the horse close together. Later he recommended only a measured advance of the hind legs under the mass of the body in order to achieve the type of collection to be suitably adopted for the practice of School horsemanship.

For us, the *rassembler* is not only a movement destined to prepare an air, nor is it only a more "engaged" attitude of the hindquarters. We consider it a general state of "concentration of the forces," or even its possibility. The impulsive thrust of the hind legs are regulated by the action of the rider's hand in the three gaits, with the possibility of reducing these gaits to null speed or even to practice any one of them backwards.

Considered this way, the *rassembler* is a general equilibrium. It facilitates the practice of these gaits on a short base, and consequently also facilitates a regulated distribution of weight between the forehand and the hindquarters in a fashion that favors this equilibrium.

The *rassembler*, as a general idea, comprises other requirements that together constitute and define it. The requirements for the forehand are the *ramener*[3], and for the hindquarters are the engagement of the hind legs, which together, correspond to what can be called the *rassembler* in a limited sense. Flexibility allows impulsion to pass from back to front by way of gymnasticized muscles and flexible joints. Lightness allows the horse to work "with only the force necessary to the movement requested."

In decomposing the *rassembler* into these elements, it is appropriate to ask if there is an order of priority to obtain this collected equilibrium.

In the first phase of his teaching, Baucher began by obtaining

---

3 The perfect vertical position of the forehead realized by a raised poll, the quasi-verticality of the forehead, and the clean definition of the parotid glands

Vulcano, sixteen years old, ridden by Dr. Ruy d'Andrade, five times older (80). Natural piaffe in lightness. Senhor d'Andrade declared that he never needed to train Vulcano.

the *ramener* and the lightness necessary for a good *mise en main*[4] with the horse at the halt. It was only then that he considered the horse apt to engage his hind legs, another requirement for the *rassembler*. The Old School (the School of Versailles) first sought the lowering of the croup, and only after that did they accept seeking the *ramener*, and the lightness of the jaw that it provoked. James Fillis practiced the *ramener* with an elevated neck with the horse in movement, whether in hand or under saddle. The Comte d'Aure, from the beginning, sought flexibility in movement, followed by the engagement of the hind legs more from the action of the hand on the bit than by increasing the activity of the hindquarters.

If we can say that the *rassembler* is the goal of dressage, that it takes a long time to be achieved, that it must be sought after patiently and methodically, then the way to attain it varies according to the constitution and temperament of each horse. It is for this reason that with some horses it will be necessary to start by conquering the hindquarters and with others by obtaining a perfect *mise en main*. In practice it will be difficult to follow a rigid rule to produce good and constant effects. Therefore the rider must exercise his tact, and have an eclectic attitude towards the writings of the masters, taking from their teachings what will serve him for the problems that he intends to solve.

4 *ramener* with a relaxed jaw

It is certain that a particular rider may have more facility in acting in a certain manner, but he must not take upon himself to only follow a single progression. From the beginning, he should seek to adapt to the circumstances by remembering that, except for rare exceptions, every horse without physical defects can be balanced. He may remember that "It is sufficient that the *écuyer* be conscious that something is possible for him to attempt it." (Baucher)

Supposing that the rider has at his disposal both forehand and hindquarters sufficiently gymnasticized? Will a simple opposition of forces be the way to bring the horse to a correct *rassembler*? And if this opposition is the best way, which technique must he use to obtain the *rassembler*?

The idea that the true *rassembler* demands a great concentration of forces was written into Baucher's First Manner, where one achieves it by using the *effet d'ensemble*[5]. We know that Baucher obtained great success with this procedure in training horses like Neptune, Buridan, Capitaine, Stades, Turban, Partisan, etc., which gave him unequalled celebrity, but we also know that this approach became the principal cause of discredit of the First Manner, according to those who had not ridden in front of the master but had only read his work. The *rassembler* of the Second Manner is obtained by alternating the *effet d'ensemble* with the "use of the leg without the hand" and of the "hand without the leg", arriving at a less pronounced concentration, but with the hind carrying more weight than the fore, while in the First Manner the weight was equally divided.

The measure of concentration of forces necessary for the *rassembler* is variable. One can see that the limit has been exceeded when the concentration of forces nullifies the disposition of the horse to carry itself forward without hesitation at whatever gait the rider wants. If that happens, it is because the concentration of forces comes too much from the *effet d'ensemble*. Consequently, the *rassembler* (at the walk, trot, or canter) is not correct because of lack of impulsion.

To attain the *rassembler*, the means may vary. But in addition to the concentration of forces that the *rassembler* requires, one must seek harmony between the forehand and the haunches, so that the impulsion is not lost. The Old School achieved the *rassembler* methodically by a progressively gymnastic process, finishing with the hindquarters

5 (effect on the whole, also called "coordinated effect", the simultaneous application of the driving and restraining aids, in such a way that the opposition of forces makes the latter annul the effects of the former completely).

Audaz, trained and ridden by Professor Jaime Celestino de Costa. Suppleness, allowing...the passage in descent of the hand...as well as the most energetic extension.

supporting the major part of the weight, with the withers lifting themselves higher than the croup.

In the first phase of Baucherism, it is not just the hind legs that approach the centre, but also the forelegs; this *rassembler* is obtained by the bringing together of all four legs. The *rassembler* of the second phase is made with the engagement of the hind legs under the body, yet they remain at a greater distance from the center than they did in the Old School. Maxime Gaussen called it, "*rassembler* without concentration of forces."

Let us see why the elements enumerated above are necessary to the *rassembler*.

Without the *ramener*, the actions of the hand are not transmitted to the hind legs. Furthermore, without a perfect position of the head realized by a raised poll, the quasi-verticality of the forehead, and the clean definition of the parotid glands in the *ramener*, the effects of the legs, especially the *attaques*[6] of the spurs, will always meet with resistance.

The engagement of the hind legs is justified by the necessity to reduce the base of support. Because the instruments of impulsion are found in the hindquarters, the domination and the mobility of the horse cannot be achieved without the practice of this engagement.

---

6 (Literally, attacks, but means repeated touches, of increasing intensity if necessary, but not violence)

Flexibility makes the horse able to move his muscles smoothly and vigorously, but without stiffening. Ease in changes of gait and direction are possible only when the loins, the spinal column, the lower jaw, etc. do not present resistance (bracing).

Total lightness is the major quality of the *rassembler*, its maximum expression. Since it is with lightness that the horse and rider are acting with minimum effort, the rider seeks to bring the horse to the point where he executes his requests almost without aids.

It is only in recognizing the necessity of these qualities that one can arrive at the concept of the *rassembler* as a general equilibrium on a short base that allows the horse to emerge from it into another more extended balance. When these balances are achieved, the flexor muscles act in maximum contraction in the *rassembler*. This contraction deploys the croup and the neck so harmoniously, putting them in a rapport such as one can see in an engraving or a photograph, that the action of the extensors (obviously predominant in the extensions) is not impeded.

If the engravings that represent the Old School positions show us the horses sitting very well, the harmony between the hindquarters and the forehand is such that the horse's disposition to forward movement does not appear in any way affected. From the beginning, Maxime Gaussen, a disciple of Baucher criticized the *rassembler* of the First Manner as being prejudicial to the impulsion because it concentrated the forces too much. He considered the *rassembler* of the Second Manner as a "*rassembler* without concentration of forces." Gaussen conceded that the best *rassembler* was that of the Old School, by reason of the harmony and balance of both ends of the horse, combined with the necessary concentration of forces. (Maxime Gaussen, *Étude sur l'Équitation Savante*, 1893).

The relative positions of the forehand and the hindquarters are very important to the collected position of the finished horse which should move with the forehand higher than the hindquarters. The difference will be more or less accentuated according to the breed of the horse. The peninsular (Iberian) horse will grow taller in the forehand, in relation to the hindquarters, than will the purebred Arabian or the Thoroughbred. The justification for this position lies in the fact that the Iberian horse is naturally more loaded on the forehand by the greater weight of his head and neck that tend to be heavier than the other breeds mentioned. That is why it is necessary to balance part of the weight toward the hindquarters, so that the horse will no longer go on the shoulders. In the natural state, the horse has too much weight on the forehand. The fundamental challenge in dressage is being able, at will, to displace toward the hindquarters the quantity of weight necessary for movement in balance.

This is in what measure?

In the first phase of his teaching, Baucher intended to distribute the weight equally between the forehand and the hindquarters. In the piaffe, the horse had to lift the forelegs to the same height as the hind legs. In his Second Manner, the same author admitted that the croup had to support more weight than the forehand, and therefore came closer to the concept of the Old School. However the Old School required a much greater difference between the fore and hind in the diagonal pair, in large part because they rode horses having pronounced knee action in the style of our peninsular horses.

**Ansioso, trained and ridden by Nuno Oliveira. Passage.
Model of relaxation and brilliance..**

The *rassembler*, as we understand it, must, whether at the walk, trot, or canter, deploy the forehand in a fashion to lift it more than the hindquarters. The hindquarters must be gymnasticized to support part of the weight of the forehand, without hindering a prompt and supple transition to more ample gaits without affecting impulsion.

In order to obtain this result, we must concern ourselves with the correctness of each of the following requirements of the *rassembler*.

THE *RAMENER*

To grasp these ideas, one could adopt the following definition: "*Ramener*, the neck raised and self-supporting, verticality of the head (or a position of the head close to the vertical, in front of it), the poll the highest point of the neck." (Decarpentry, *Piaffer et Passage*, 1932, p. 9.) The *ramener* is integrated into School Horsemanship as one of the fundamental requirements of the *rassembler*. It is an incomplete requirement. It must be linked to the *rassembler's* other characteristics of which we have already spoken.

The simple notion of *ramener*, such as we have described above, is acceptable for other branches of horsemanship. But in High School, it is intimately connected to that of lightness, producing what we call the *mise en main*[7], and to that of flexibility, by requiring of the horse a position of the forehead close to the vertical by the flexion of the first two vertebrae of the neck, and an engagement of the hind legs, putting the end of the nose at a higher level than the hip joint. Even if this ideal *ramener* cannot always be obtained, we must know which goal we seek in our work. It is only when the head attains verticality and the horse achieves lightness, in which a clean definition of the parotids[8] is produced. Only then can we consider the forehand to be in an academic position.

Let us recap the advantages of the *ramener* as it applies to the demands of the *rassembler*, and thus of School Horsemanship:

1. It helps the engagement of the hind legs and favors the supple action of the back and the loins.

2. Accompanied by the relaxation of the jaw (*mise en main*), it

---

7 Relaxation of the jaw; putting the horse in the hand
8 The pair of salivary glands situated below and in front of each ear

allows all the actions of the hand to be transmitted to all parts of the body and vise-versa, predisposing the mouth to receive the impulsion coming from the hindquarters as well as all actions of the rider's legs.

3. The verticality of the forehead , or slightly in front of the vertical position, even when not accompanied by the relaxation of the jaw, facilitates the regularity of the gaits. Because they know that, the circus trainers strongly tighten the fixed side-reins until the forced position of the head becomes habitual, and the horses cadence themselves.

4. The *ramener* is undeniably an extraordinary means of domination, whether it is obtained delicately by the hand, with lightness in the mouth, or if it is forced by fixed side reins (in the pillars or on the longe), or "by the vigor of the rider's legs pushing the forces onto the bit against which resistances dissolve." (Beudant, *Souvenirs Équestres*, 1934, p. 52.)

5. "When capable of giving the *mise en main*, the horse can even tolerate a sudden movement of the hand without feeling the discomfort that would result if the horse is stiff." (Wachter, *Aperçus Équestres*, 1862, p. 10.);

6. As L'Hotte says (*Questions Équestres*, 1906, p. 117.), "A long neck, instead of being light, puts more weight on the shoulders than a neck that is thick but short, and that its changes in position bring about displacement of weight that are much more noticeable." Only the *ramener* can cause a part of this weight to be carried by the hindquarters, bringing the centre of gravity back by shortening the ensemble of the neck and head. General Decarpentry expresses the same idea in describing the "regular stance" prescribed by Raabe (*L'Essentiel de la Méthode de Haute École de Raabe*, 1957, p. 107.): "In this position, two thirds of the weight of the rider adds to the natural surcharge on the shoulders. The horse has therefore a tendency to 'fall on the front' if the *ramener* does not intervene in the inverse direction, by bringing back the centre of gravity resulting from the shortening imposed on the ensemble of the neck and the head."

7. The vertical position of the head connects to the contact that the rider should have with the horse's bit. Dupaty de Clam wrote, "The perpendicular line of the horse's face is the unique position

in which the contact with the hand is felt correctly, and it is in this position that the support[9] (of the hand) becomes perfect." (*Practique de l'Équitation*, 1769, p. 75.)

In summary "...it is certain, and I will give all the proof that one could want, that all parts of the horse's body are organized by the position of the neck and the head." (Baron de Sind, *L'Art du Manège*, 1774, p. 15.)

In enumerating the requirements of the *rassembler*, we begin with the *ramener* as did Baucher, the opposite of the Old School who considered it a consequence of the engagement of the hindquarters.

We believe that Baucher was right when proceeding by *partial actions*[10], and beginning with the "placer" (positioning) of the front end[11]. In effect the horse's neck is not "attached", so to speak, to the dorsal vertebrae. The horse does not have clavicles. There is a muscular cradle with a little elasticity between the shoulder blades[12] that supports the withers. We think of the top line of the horse as divided into two parts: one in front, and the other behind the withers.

If the horse's head is lifted above its normal position, the vertebrae of the neck weigh on that cradle of muscles. The attempted engagement of the hindquarters that this positioning provokes is obtained at the price of pushing the withers down, with a hollow stiffening of the back, and a rising of the croup. This "placer" is therefore harmful.

It is appropriate to position the forehand in a way that the muscles supporting the withers come up as much as possible. In the pursuit of this goal, a lowering of the neck with a somewhat "long" *ramener* (a longer, lowered neck), is not only to be advised as a general rule, but is even indispensable in many cases. When the forehand is positioned in a way that facilitates the raising of the withers, the withers will muscle up. Meanwhile the gymnasticising of the hindquarters (to be practiced later on according to the Baucherist concept) will complete the work, consistent with placing the withers in such a way that it facilitates the transmission of the actions of the hand down along the vertebrae of the neck and the back, and reciprocally, the actions of the hindquarters up to the horse's mouth.

---

9   *appui*
10   (gymnastic)
11   (neck and head)
12   (scapulae)

The trot. "By the trot... acquire suppleness of the first degree."
Andrade, 1790.

The trot.
"The exercise that with discretion improves the horse's *ressorts* (springs, joints, resources)."
Dupaty, 1776.

THE ENGAGEMENT OF THE HIND LEGS

This engaged position of the hindquarters is absolutely necessary. It alone will allow the domination of the horse, the rapid movements in every direction, and the impulsion necessary for the exercises of the School Horsemanship and the brilliance of the airs.

The rational explanation of the necessity to engage the hindquarters is found in the study of "the balance of superimposed bodies" according to Raabe (p. 138 in Decarpentry's book): "The equilibrist who places a peacock feather standing up on his nose is moving his base of support at every instant to keep the feather in balance and to prevent it from falling. The feather, by its various inclinations, compels the man to walk so that he can keep supporting it."

"The same phenomenon is produced by the rider when the horse is maintained in a sufficiently complete *rassembler*. It suffices for the rider to tip his upper body very slightly to drive the parallel forces created by the weight of the rider's leaning body in all directions, as it also suffices for him to re-establish vertical straightness in a static position to immobilize the horse."

Given this explanation, one well understands that, as Raabe also wrote, "the resistance coming from the horse is in direct relation to the increase of the surface of his base of support." For all that, this truth could make one suppose that the reduction in the base of support should be obtained by bringing both the hind and forelegs under the body, to the end that the sought-after reduction is made by all four legs.

However, we seek balance on a diminished base. Narrowing of the base is required by the *rassembler*. It is produced by the progressive advance of the hindquarters under the body, and not by the combination of this advance with the drawing back of the forelegs behind their normal vertical line.

Even though Baucher's First Manner was practiced in this position, the advantages that it might have presented were a lot fewer than its inconveniences, especially the prejudice that it carried against impulsion. This does not mean to say that the *rassembler* of a Baucherised horse of 1842 should not be applied to certain horses, since it gives the horse's back great flexibility. However, it was difficult to measure, and if it were ill-practiced, it was very dangerous. (It is probable that the master himself escaped danger, if one were to judge by the famous engravings representing Baucher on Partisan in piaffe. It dates from 1840.)

The academic concentration of forces requires that the base of support formed by the horse's legs be shortened by the engagement of the hindquarters under the body. That is why we have made this engagement a requirement in the *rassembler*.

Of course the engagement of the hindquarters exists in many other positions that are less collected than the school position: at the moment of a jump, a rapid pirouette in front of a bull, in the pasture grazing, jumping straight up before bucking, or even in lying down. In each of these examples, the horse flexes his hindquarters. But it is only in the true *rassembler* that the engagement of the hindquarters is combined with the other elements that we are studying (the *ramener*), and it is only in this way that one can achieve a position of balance, when they are all brought together.

FLEXIBILITY

By flexibility, we understand the facility of the joints that allows them to activate the horse and enables him to pass without a jolt, but with promptness, from short to ample gaits and vice versa.

The flexibility that the horse should possess by nature is what the *écuyer* must seek to give him if the horse is not especially gifted. The result is called academic impulsion.

Normal impulsion is "necessary to obtaining any movement, just like steam pressure is necessary to the machine, whatever the direction of its work" (Saint Phalle, *Équitation, Tome II,* 1907, p. 20). But for the changes of direction, the horse must be sufficiently flexible.

One must not confuse impulsion with speed, or with the simple propensity of the horse to go forward.

The impulsion of academic dressage is a consequence of the general flexibility of the horse, the result of contraction and *decontraction* (relaxation) of muscles so that the rider can have this facility at his disposal both laterally and longitudinally.

The impulsive horse will be "under pressure." The "pressure" of that impulsion can be used in the nimbleness of the lengthening of the gait, in the height of the airs on a short base, and in the gaits executed backwards, if they are practiced with energy and calm, preserving the horse's tendency for forward movement, without haste, but with keenness.

Many horses do not possess the constitution to tolerate the gymnastic bending that leads to superior impulsion. An *écuyer* deserving of the name will seek to develop any deficient muscles in horses. It is in relation to the flexibility of the back that one distinguishes between a horse that "walks with his back" and one that "walk with his legs." The dorsal spine transmits the impulsion from the hindquarters to the horse's mouth through the hand of the rider.

In *L'Éperon* of February 1957, M. Glahn wrote that "before the First World War, the principal criterion (for judging a horse) was that he possess the ability to use his back in an elastic manner. It was the standard notion of all the 'protocols,' of all the critiques, of all the reports."

One reads sometimes that a certain presentation was excellent. But first, I am obliged to say what constitutes excellence. Is it only to have

**Counter shoulder-in on the circle.
"It is with flexibility and a soft enveloping that one succeeds: force disconcerts the horse and fatigues him in excess."**
Dupaty, 1776.

executed a reprise (test) without errors? To judge a ride excellent says nothing if it applies to a horse who executed the program in an automatic manner, using his legs without employing the rest of his body. But it says everything if it applies to a horse whose back is active and flexible, even if the horse does not yet know how to respond to every request, such as the position and the flexions.

Because he was preoccupied with the flexibility of the back, Baucher, in his First Manner, brought his horses' hind legs and forelegs together almost to the point of joining them. General L'Hotte, speaking of the impulsion transmitted up to the hand by a very flexible back, said that the rider felt it "as undulations resembling a sheet of water passing under his seat."

It may seem strange that we have used the title: flexibility, and not "impulsion." But, as we have already said, impulsion must derive from flexibility. Otherwise, it would be defective in light of the criteria by which

Canter to the right.
Dupaty, 1776
"The rassembler of the Old School deploys the neck flexors so harmoniously in relation to those of the croup that this position is no obstacle to forward movement."
Diogo de Bragança

we appreciate academic dressage.

Let us take an example: observe a horse that passages with energy and brilliance so that the rider is bounced by the horse's back at each beat of the passage. The horse is executing the air with energy, but lacks flexibility, and the rider is not successfully connecting to the movement of his mount. The horse is animated by only an elementary impulsion, because that impulsion is not accompanied by the necessary flexibility. Therefore, this example cannot be considered the impulsion of good school horsemanship. (L'Hotte, *Questions Équestres*, 1906, p. 27).

This same author wrote comparing d'Aurism and Baucherism (*Un Officier de Cavalerie*, 1905, p. 249.): "Like d'Aure, Baucher called upon impulsion right away, but instead of letting it immediately escape forward, he wanted the rider first to hold it to get the submission of the springs (joints)."

D'Aure's system used impulsion directly so that the horse would be "forward," as he said constantly to his students. Baucher used impulsion to vanquish all resistances, which little by little must yield in the rider's hand (*effet d'ensemble*). Baucher's preoccupation is reflected in his advice to "push." In comparing the two systems in which these celebrated masters used impulsion, one arrives at the conclusion that d'Aure used it purely and simply in forward movement, while Baucher used it to obtain the flexibility of different parts of the horse (*partial actions*) so that this impulsion would be thereafter available "in the fashion of a cherry pit that squirts under the pressure of the fingers." (Paul de Courtivron, cited by L'Hotte, *Un Officier...* 1905, p. 248) I think that it is this latter manner of using impulsion -- the kind that derives from total flexibility -- that is beneficial for balance in high level dressage.

My opinion on this subject is corroborated by an observation by D. José Manuel da Cunha Menezes. He reported in the review *Ano Hipico Portugues* (1954): "...natural impulsion, when associated with the general difficulties of the mouth contributes powerfully to the deviation of the croup from its regular position relative to the shoulders. I do not know if it has already been remarked that horses that are less energetic and easy in their mouths deviate the least from the correct position." And why? Because they are more flexible.

Only flexibility renders impulsion controllable to the point of allowing the practice and domination required by *Haute École*. That is why we consider it an element of the *rassembler*.

LIGHTNESS

True lightness allows one to employ only the force necessary for the production of a requested movement. Lightness is understood as referring first to the relaxation of the jaw, and then to the mobility of the haunches. Strictly speaking one could say that these two expressions of the word "lightness" are two ways of envisioning its manifestations. So if lightness of the jaw is transmitted to the cervical vertebrae and to the rest of the spinal column, likewise the lightness of the haunches has repercussions to the mouth, and provokes relaxation of the jaw.

The Old School considered lightness to be a consequence of the general flexibility of the horse. Baucher considered lightness the effect of this flexibility as well as its cause.[13]

---

13 This concept, so pertinent, is marvelously clarified by these few lines written by Georges Duhamel at the death of Professor Leriche in December 1955: "The doctors of my generation have been wisely brought up in the idea that, to make the ef-

In truth, in a well-conformed horse, lightness results from general equilibrium. But to obtain lightness in those with conformation faults, it is necessary – since these faults tend to manifest in the mouth – to address the local suppling of the lower jaw. One cannot hope that lightness will be the result of general equilibrium given when the latter is deficient.

True lightness is very difficult to obtain. Most of the time we encounter situations that create alternately varying degrees of relaxation and *appui* (heavy contact). These attitudes vary between those of "*bavard*[14]" horses (agitated mouths) in false lightness, and those of horses that execute the demanded exercises correctly, all the while remaining mute and contracted. Once again, it is necessary to say that "the wisdom is in finding the right balance." General L'Hotte wrote, "The horse that is satisfactorily light should be neither mute nor *bavard.*"

L'Hotte teaches that lightness of the jaw should be manifested only when it is requested. "...it is necessary that its soft loosening, that should only be a slight murmur, is produced in the course of work, at the first call of the hand, only to cease as soon as there is not longer cause for it." (*Questions Équestres*, 1906, p. 36.)

Except for the respect owed to him , this instruction from L'Hotte cannot be taken too literally by anyone who considers lightness indispensable to the *rassembler* of academic dressage. In a judged presentation according to academic criteria, it would not be practical to have an interruption of lightness in the horse. The *écuyer* must train the horse to a permanent state of total relaxation, which is not compatible with the need for the intervention of the hand every time there is a loss of lightness, precisely because the hand has ceased to act.

To achieve perfection, the rider must put into practice Baucher's teaching - "make him understand, and let him do it" – leading to the descent of hand and leg (yielding of the aids) characterizing the perfect attitude of *Haute École* in which the horse is led to work in freedom; that is, so to speak, "on parole."

---

fect disappear, it was, in good logic, necessary to remove the cause. René Leriche, master doctor and pain specialist had the very surprising idea to treat certain kinds of suffering by attacking them directly by analgesic injections. This admirable treatment, theoretically symptomatic, often produced a curative effect. The effect removed the cause, believe it or not, which found itself sent on vacation. It faded away and disappeared." (Note of the French Translator)

14 Literally: talkative,(moving the mouth excessively)

Why is lightness considered the hallmark of School horsemanship?

Because "lightness is the perfect obedience of the horse to the lightest indications of the hand and heels of his rider...it finds its formulation in the action of the rider putting into play, and the horse using, only the force necessary to the movement envisioned. Any other manifestation of force is likely to produce a resistance, and consequently, an alteration of lightness." (L'Hotte, *Questions Équestres*, 1906, pp. 33, 34).

This means that perfection cannot be attained if there is any jerkiness, loss of cadence, or loss of muscular relaxation. Only lightness that gives the horse a natural position without apparent effort is the proof of perfect balance.

To return to the question of knowing whether it is lightness or the *rassembler* that characterizes *Haute École*, we can now conclude that it is the latter that, in truth, is its mark. When Baucher said that lightness is as much a cause as an effect, he was referring to the lightness of the jaw. As a cause, it can contribute to obtaining a good balance, that is to say the *rassembler*. As an effect, it can be the consequence of the *rassembler*. In saying that lightness characterizes School Horsemanship, I am referring to the minimum effort necessary for the rider to obtain an action by his horse -- a force exactly adjusted to what the rider wants of him. But for this to happen, the horse must be in *rassembler*. There are trained horses, of which the rider has demanded a *rassembler* with pressure (*appui*) on the bit, who execute correct airs, but without lightness. They lack the *coquetterie* [15] that the rider must impart to his mount in helping him give the impression that all that he is doing is natural, however complicated it may be.

Rassembler without lightness exists in well-trained horses in School Horsemanship. Some of the horses of the School of Vienna, and the majority of German horses present *rassembler* without maximum lightness. However, lightness gives *rassembler* its greatest value. Lightness ennobles it, and finally, confers on the *rassembler* the artistic quality that it must have.

---

15 playfulness

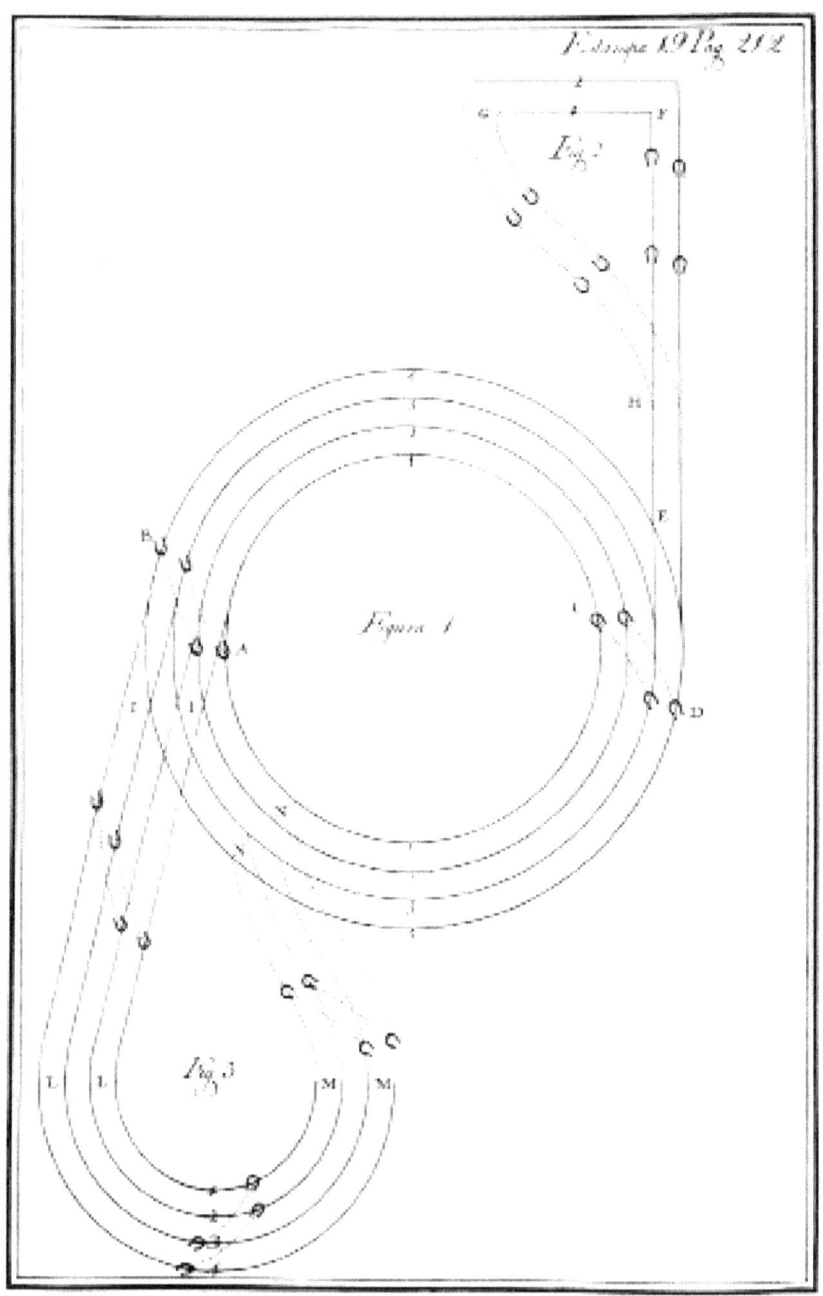

Circles on four tracks to the left and change of hand.

CHAPTER 2

LIMITS OF THE *RASSEMBLER*

Would it be advantageous for academic dressage to practice the maximum *rassembler* that each horse could support? To go to the limit of the *ramener*? Of the engagement of the hindquarters? Of flexibility? Of lightness? I will examine each of these points.

LIMITS OF THE *RAMENER*

Most authors consider that a good *ramener* is one with the horse's forehead vertical or at a slight incline in front of the vertical. They condemn an incline behind the vertical as a certain sign of *acculement*[16]. For these authors, the limit of the *ramener* is verticality. But if a position behind the vertical by itself is not a manifestation of *acculement*, and if otherwise the horse responds diligently to the leg, this position might be necessary to balance certain individual horses with low set or upside-down necks, weak hindquarters, long backs, or weak loins. This position of the head and neck lightens the hindquarters by allowing the horse to shift part of the weight to the forehand. On the subject of the position behind the vertical that one must give to certain horses, such as with many Iberian horses with weak hindquarters and withers much higher than the croup, Baucher wrote (*Méthode d'Équitation basée sur de nouveaux principes, 6ᵉ éd*. 1844, p. 193, note I): "In effect, one is then obliged, in order to render the horse's movement uniform, to lower the neck so that the sort of lever arm that it represents serves to relieve the weight with which the hindquarters find themselves overloaded."

I believe the limit of the *ramener* can be achieved with the head behind the vertical when this position facilitates the acquisition of an equilibrium that is susceptible to being maintained at all gaits.

True academic dressage must seek impulsion coming from the hindquarters, in transmitting through the back and along all of the

---

16 (Holding back, backing, "sucking back," horse "back on his heels," "behind the bit" or "behind the leg")

vertebrae of the neck up to the mouth. If the impulsion does not reach the first vertebra because the hand has intervened at the wrong time, the neck takes on the shape of a "pigeon throat" (protruding under neck muscle), or the horse overflexes. The direction of the impulsion becomes irregular and difficult to control. With the *ramener* vertical, or in certain cases, behind the vertical, one obtains mastery of impulsion. It is passed all along the vertebrae of the back and neck to arrive at the jaw without impeding the supple and regular functioning of the spinal column as the transmitter of the action created by the hind legs. The gymnasticising of the loins finds itself facilitated, and its work eased.

Certain actions of the hands, such as vibrations and especially *"demi-arêtes"* (half-halts), require a complete *ramener*. Since the conformation of certain horses requires placing the head behind the vertical, these effects of the reins only produce the desired result if such a position of the head has been already obtained. In fact, the half-halt will only annul a resistance of weight by shifting it from the forehand to the hindquarters if the medium of transmission is in a state conducive to this shift. In a similar case, therefore, the rider can only make the horse *"remonter sur la main*[17]*"* if his head is vertical or slightly behind the vertical.

While the *ramener* has an ideal limit in the verticality of the head, that does not mean that during training one might not have need to place the head in other than the final position, whether it be a more pronounced direct flexion, or the maximum lateral flexion of the jaw and neck, or the more or less prolonged practice of the *ramener outré*[18].

I have seen, as many others have remarked, international jumping champions, Winkler, Thiedemann, and their teammates use very tight side-reins in preparation for the round they would be riding immediately afterward. This demonstrates that many times one must pass through preliminary positions of the head, according to the horse, towards the end of creating obedience to the rider's hand repeatedly. Then one can achieve the free play of the neck, back, and hindquarters to allow conservation of the desired balance. The majority of contemporary writers do not recommend the practice of many variations of the *ramener*. But older authors, conscious of the means and powers of

---

17 "the horse coming back up on the hand"--essentially a half-halt with a flexion of the neck, raising of the withers, and an engagement of the hindquarters (Oliveira, *Œuvres Complètes*, Belin, Paris, 2006, p. 100)
18 (exaggerated, behind the vertical)

training, taught these variations, and persuaded that they supported effectiveness in "placing" horses with defective conformation. For example, *Pellier fils* wrote (*L'Équitation practique, 3ᵉ éd.* 1875, p. 113.): "To arrive at this end (the *ramener*), if the horse has his nose in the wind, you look to place it at first a little behind the perpendicular." And Gerhardt (*Manuel d'Équitation*, 1859, p. 81.): "As to horses that resist downwards and those that ... look to escape the pressure (*pression*) of the bit, lifting the head to force against the hand, the rider flexes them downward until the resistance has disappeared."

While defending the foregoing ideas concerning the means of getting to a perfect *ramener*, I do not pretend to condemn those who think that it should be obtained by the relaxation of the jaw on an elevated neck with the head even horizontal. But I do believe that this position is not applicable to the majority of horses because it tends to sink the withers, and in consequence does not facilitate the proper work of the vertebrae in the transmission of impulsion. I am in accord with General Decarpentry (*L'Essentiel de la Méthode de Haute École de Raabe*, 1957, p. 148.) In this book, he prefers momentary actions of elevating the hand as a means to half-halt on a single rein affected only on the convex side of the neck. These actions also allow the rider to obtain a purely local mobilization of the jaw.

LIMITS OF THE ENGAGEMENT OF THE HINDQUARTERS

The *rassembler* is not only the characteristic of academic equilibrium. It is also an extraordinary means of domination. By obtaining the submission of the instruments of impulsion ("the engine of the horse,") the rassembler makes the engagement of the hindquarters easy.

The advancement of the hind legs under the body reduces the base of support thereby contributing to a greater mobility of the horse-rider ensemble (theory of superimposed bodies). It allows perhaps an even more advantageous result: the absolute control of the will of the horse, "until it becomes one" with the rider, in the words of Raabe. (Decarpentry, *L'Essentiel de la Méthode de Haute École de Raabe*, 1957, p. 135.)

Not every horse can give us the same degree of concentration of the hindquarters over the course of training. The degree of engagement of the hindquarters, by which we seek to dominate the horse, differs greatly according to each individual rider. It is related to his physical and moral constitution.

One must distinguish the concentration as a means of domination, a normal procedure in dressage, from the engagement which ennobles the airs, giving them correctness and brilliance. The first purpose must go to the limit of the faculties of the horse in order to obtain absolute command. The second aims at perfection beyond and short of which the work becomes incorrect.

For example, the piaffe must fulfill the same conditions to be correct for any horse, regardless of breed. But the degree of concentration of the hindquarters, practiced as a gymnastic, varies a great deal according to the horse's constitution and "blood." Without having obtained the maximum possible engagement of the hindquarters, the rider cannot say that his mount is in total submission.

This question presents the greatest interest as it applies to horses capable of a natural engagement, greater than the perfection of an air would demand. Such was produced with the horses ridden by the Old School riders and is still the case today with Iberian breeds. For example, the piaffe demanded of these horses is executed with requisite effort regarding engagement (the hocks up to the vertical line drawn down from the point of the haunches). But if the horse is powerful and hot and the rider has not made him practice maximum engagement, and has not required him to accept this engagement at any moment, the total domination of the horse can not be achieved.

There is a difference between the engagement of the hindquarters used as an element of domination and that engagement which the horse must achieve in a presentation. Most riders practicing current competition dressage appear to forget about this problem of domination. They confine themselves to obtaining only as much concentration as is required by the airs that they have to practice in a dressage test, and so their horses give the impression of being able to evade from the immediate obedience that the rider should have required.

Our bullfighting riders are required to bring their mounts to a supreme degree of engagement, precisely because they need immediate domination in the voltes, pirouettes, rein-backs, sudden departs and halts in their "fight" with the bulls. Only practice of sufficient concentration makes the quiet execution of these airs possible. Peninsular horses

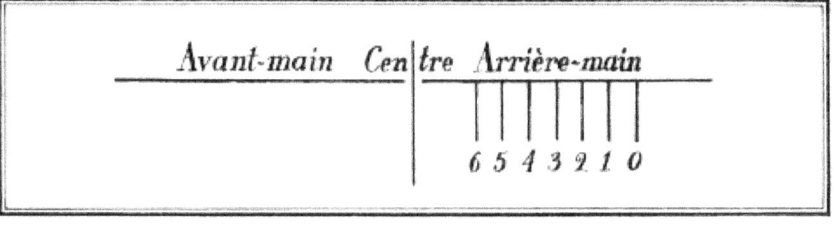

(Forehand   Center   Hind legs)

make us understand this problem clearly. They have more facility than any other horses in working "on their haunches." Tauromachic horsemanship is inspired by the "sitting" position of the Old School horses. Let us explain by means of a diagram. (Baucher, *Méthode d'Équitation*, 14ᵉ éd. 1874, p. 124.)

For example, if we want to consider any horse trained in the piaffe, he must attain engagement of the hindquarters up to point 3. While there are horses that have trouble getting to this point, there are those who easily get to point 5 on the accompanying diagram.

With the first type, one arrives at the concentration necessary in this air only by a prudent training progression full of tact. A horse of the second type can take a sitting position very well beyond the requirements of the piaffe.

To review, there are horses whose maximum engagement is the attainment of the school airs required in today's dressage tests – piaffe, passage, pirouettes. But there are also horses whose *rassembler* greatly surpasses that required in these tests.

Is it necessary, to approach the maximum engagement of the hindquarters of which each horse is capable? According to Raabe (Decarpentry, *L'Essentiel...*, 1957, p. 145.), "The more the rider can require the horse to bring together his four legs, the more he obliges him to use his forces in a manner indispensable to remain in balance, the more the equilibrium becomes sensitive to the least displacement of weight."

If we do not put this teaching into practice, horses that are difficult to collect[19] (which cannot attain point 3 easily) will not get to the maximum level of concentration necessary for obtaining the airs required in today's dressage tests. Furthermore those who attain point

---

19 *rassembler*

5 by themselves will not be absolutely dominated. When a horse which attains point 5 (engagement of the hindquarters) easily by himself is *rassemblé* only to point 3 (engagement of the hindquarters necessary to the execution of the air), it could happen that he would use his own faculty to sit down immediately on the hindquarters to evade the demand of his rider, and the rider would then lose control of his horse.

Baucher's First Manner *rassembler*, as it has been represented with the fore and hind legs approaching each other, has been criticized as a position that is a distortion of good dressage. Yet if we make clear the distinction that I will set out, this *rassembler* finds its justification.

We should not presume that this genius rider practiced piaffe with the horse risking stepping on its own feet. The profile of a Baucherised horse at the beginning of the First Manner actually represents a concentrated position that exercises and dominates the horse, and prepares him for the correct execution of piaffe at the end of his training.

It is said that the Portuguese Master Vitorino Frois spent the major part of a lesson practicing the position of "a mountain goat on a peak," and although this position has been accused of extinguishing the horse's movement, to this day we still speak of the brilliance with which this celebrated Tauromachic rider's mounts worked.

What explains this apparent contradiction is that, as I have shown, the practice of engagement of the hindquarters, as an exercise that gymnasticizes and dominates, is different from the final *rassembler* for which it prepares, the first acting until the maximum engagement to which the horse consents is achieved, and the second adjusting itself exactly to the engagement required by the rules of dressage.

I believe that this is one of the reasons that the modern dressage tests demand piaffe, passage, pirouettes, and changes every stride, without considering the utility of the maximum engagement of the hindquarters under the mass to which any given horse is capable. Considering only the *rassembler* called for by the air that a rider wishes to perform, and not applying himself to the one required for the domination of the horse, the trainer reaches the point of fearing that the horse, through excess engagement, will ruin the good execution of a test.

Modern dressage tends to consider the pronounced lowering of the haunches as a fault and has concluded that the old airs for which this

Croup to the wall (renvers, haunches out).
"... the horse takes on little by little the habit of going in a bend, and of looking in the direction that he is going while moving to the side."
La Guérinière, 1733.

lowering was required do not present interest. It even seems that it they are no longer even considered. The regulation of the FEI states (par. 420) "The School jumps, abandoned in a great number of countries, do not figure, for this reason, in the program of the Grand Prix."

The reason invoked appears to have very little value, because if these airs were required, or simply authorized by the FEI, they would mark the continuation of a form of dressage of unequaled beauty in the greatest tradition. Why do the tests not contain a part in which the rider is not required to submit to an obligatory program, but rather be able to show the airs that his inspiration and the possibilities of his horse permit, for example: pirouette in piaffe, passage to the rear, canter in place? The current School horsemanship appears condemned to die of monotony!

The underlying reason for which these airs are not admitted is the consequence of what we have written about above. The more a horse is collected to execute a figure of the *manège*, the more he puts himself on the haunches. But the movements practiced today demand only a little pronounced lowering of the haunches. The efficacy and solidity of true dressage are found to be seriously compromised.

It is nearly certain that the question of the bending of the haunches has not been taken into consideration by the FEI, because horses from the Iberian Peninsula are practically unknown, or judged to be without interest for international tests.

Since we think that true dressage must resolve the double problem of domination and balance in all horses, we have laid out these reflections suggested to us by the balance that the peninsular horse takes up so easily under his rider. These reflections, based on the natural tendencies of the peninsular horse, do not discount the training of horses of other breeds as more difficult or easy.

LIMITS OF FLEXIBILITY

We have described our idea of flexibility, and by connecting it to the superior impulsion required by academic dressage, we have made it dependant on the horse's natural tendency to forward movement with suppleness in the functioning of his joints.

The limit of flexibility is attained when the horse will no longer accept to go forward in the requested gait. This is what is happening if the horse, chomping his bit to excess while at the halt, departs at the canter when the trot or the walk have been requested. The rider can be sure that the mobility of the jaw has been brought to the point of exaggeration. Another example: If the trainer wants his mount to halt perfectly, but the horse engages and mobilizes his hindquarters, putting himself into what one could call "agitated halt," we must conclude that the flexibility of the hindquarters has been pushed too far.

If again the *rassembler* is apparently correct, but at a request for lengthening, the horse does not respond whether because he holds back, or he hurries his stride, losing coordination, it is proof that the flexibility acquired with the *rassembler* was pushed to excess, etc.

In practice, flexibility is a faculty of the horse that is available to the rider to control impulsion. Impulsion can be defined as the desire of the horse to carry himself forward. It is an essential quality in the mounted horse. It is the "forward" of General L'Hotte. In academic dressage, the problem of impulsion affects the rider's total control of the horse in every direction, at any gait, in all transitions. How is this domination obtained? By the flexibility given to the joints that are moved by muscles made strong and elastic by appropriate gymnastics.

While flexibility is a requirement of the *rassembler*, and thus of superior dressage, it must not harm the results obtained by elementary dressage, and so never injure the characteristics that have allowed one to obtain a horse that is calm, straight, and full of impulsion.

Flexibility has the goal of making the horse so handy that he will be able to advance, halt, rein-back, and move laterally with the greatest of ease, but without ever harming the impulsion of the gait requested by the rider. That is the limit of flexibility!

LIMITS OF LIGHTNESS

In its largest sense, lightness signifies the general state of relaxation that allows a horse to work with only the effort necessary to a movement in the course of its execution. In its limited sense, which is the more common one, the word is applied correctly to the ease with which the yielding of the jaw, and the bending of the haunches, are produced.

In its first sense, lightness is without limit. It is what the French School considers perfection, the quintessence of *Haute École*, where the horse works with minimum effort in response to the mildest of aids. The sole limit that one could perhaps assign to lightness would be the simultaneous descent of the hand and legs, the supreme refinement of "*l'équitation savante*.[20]" Faverot de Kerbrech considered that airs are perfect when they are executed with the reins on the neck, without intervention of the legs, according to the doctrine of the last teaching of Baucher, which illustrates a liberty conceded to horses only comparable to those which Rousselet practiced instinctively.

As "Rousselet presented himself above all as the successor to the traditions of the past" (L'Hotte, *Un Officier de Cavalerie*, 1905, p. 352.) and if Baucher, in his last manner, gave the horse a liberty characteristic of the work of that same gentle *écuyer* and the school that he represented,

Furtif, trained and ridden by René Bacharach in 1955. Appuyer (half-pass) left at the trot. Collection, lightness, crossing, parallelism, engagement. "This age old truth that the horse goes better all on his own."
— John Paget.

Appuyer right in trot. "Moving away from the left leg, the pli (bend) is to the right."
Aubert, 1836.

20 Learned horsemanship

and if we recall that the *écuyers:* L'Hotte, Faverot de Kerbrech, Beudant...left their mounts function in a system of liberty on parole[21], we can conclude that lightness, in its largest sense, is undoubtedly characteristic of the French School of academic dressage.

In its limited sense, the concept of lightness, seen as the ease with which the jaw yields, or the quickness with which the haunches obey the rider, has a limit. The flexibility of the joints of the jaw and the haunches must be developed as necessary, but not to the point where suppleness becomes weakness.

In the time of the School of Versailles, they had already been saying that "to make a perfect *écuyer* requires the legs of Monsieur de La Bigne and the hand of Monsieur d'Abzac." This shows that the degree of lightness is evaluated by the ease with which the rider engages the jaw and the haunches of his horses. It is for no other reason that Baucher founded his method on *partial actions* (independence of the gymnastic flexions of all the joints), a means of working with a degree of effort that is exactly proportional to the movement demanded. This is the height of the expression of academic dressage, as was brilliantly explained by General L'Hotte.

Commandant de Salins said, "Lightness is only limited by the tact of the rider."

---

21 A degree of freedom based on a the goodwill of the horse to fulfill the rider's request "as of his own idea."

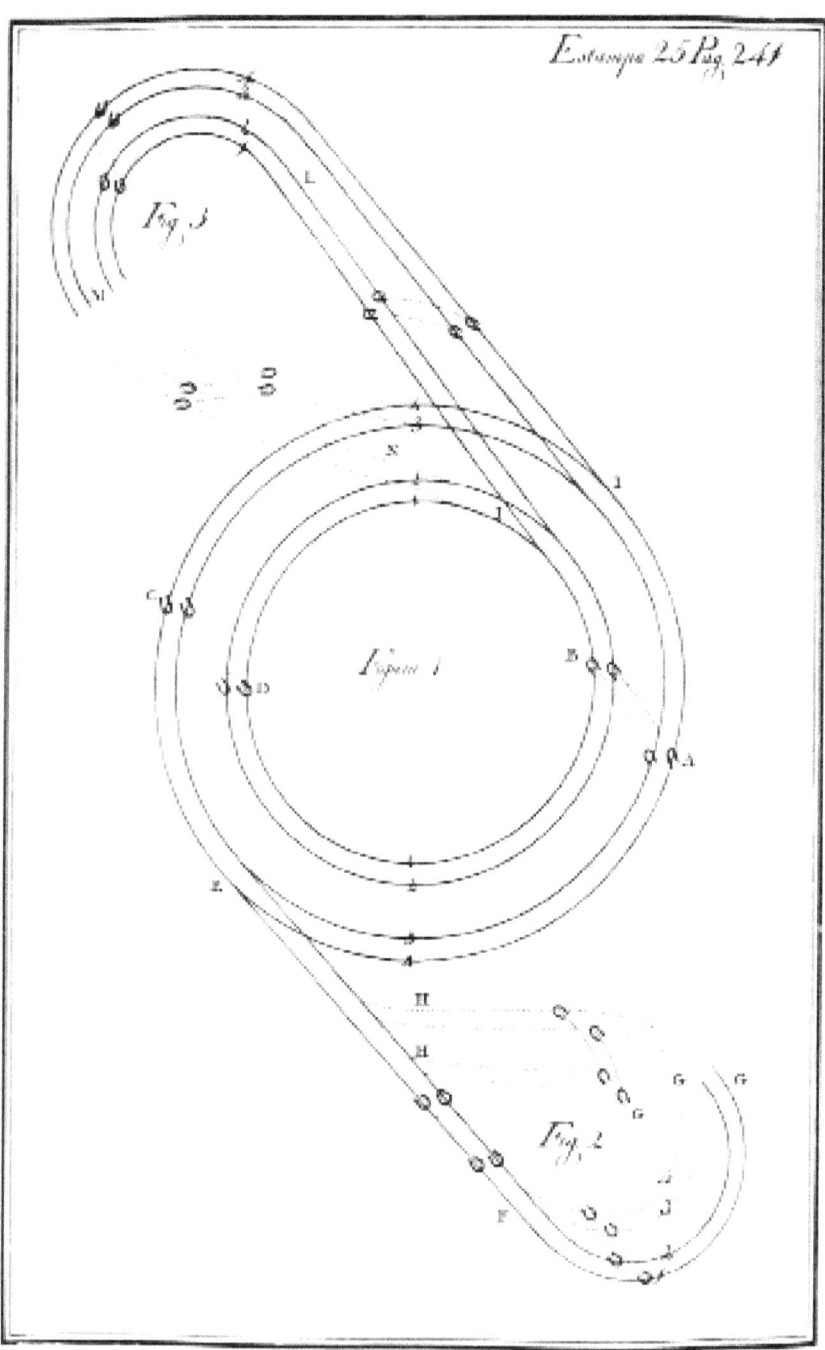

Lesson of four circles in the canter to the left.

PART TWO

SYSTEMS OF HORSEMANSHIP

A new system of horsemanship appears each time a new type of horse, characterized by his morphology and his temperament, in other words, a new breed, comes into common usage, or when a new way of using the horse is introduced. It is evident that changes due to the first of these causes are infrequent. A breed for common use in a given equestrian milieu varies only imperceptibly. But if a breed totally different from one that had been in use until then comes into fashion, the method used to resolve the equestrian problems that this new breed poses must have an original character in order to adapt to the constitution of the new type of horse. So, without denying the work of Xenophon, King Duarte I of Portugal, de Fiaschi, La Broue, or Pluvinel, who brought to their eras very notable progress on the road to perfecting equestrian art, one could say that among the works that merit the name of methods, properly speaking, are first those that attains its best known expression in La Guérinère, then that of François Baucher. They were connected, one to the fashion for a short, strong horse with rounded movement that sat on his haunches, typified by the Iberian horse, and the other to the vogue in France for the English thoroughbred in the first half on the XIX century. The necessity for Baucher's method made itself felt in the new problems that resulted when *écuyers* wanted to submit the thoroughbred to academic dressage, because the rules of the Old School showed themselves to be of difficult application and uncertain effect.

This does not mean to say that there were not many personal methods or "progressions" available. But they were all inspired more or less by one or the other of these two great systems, according to the modality called for by the horsemanship envisioned. It is in this way, for example, that d'Auvergne simplified the method of Montfaucon de Rogles to apply it to military horsemanship, and that Count d'Aure did in the same way with the teaching of Viscount d'Abzac, so that his techniques would be applicable to "*campagne* equitation" (cross country). On the other hand, the teachings of Raabe, Fillis, Decarpentry, or Jousseaume are inspired by Baucher's doctrine, explaining his methodology in a better way or giving his progression a better order, to solve the problems posed by academic dressage. By analyzing, even summarily, the Old School methods and those of Baucher, we have an idea of the equestrian procedures that have had the most influence on the history of horsemanship.

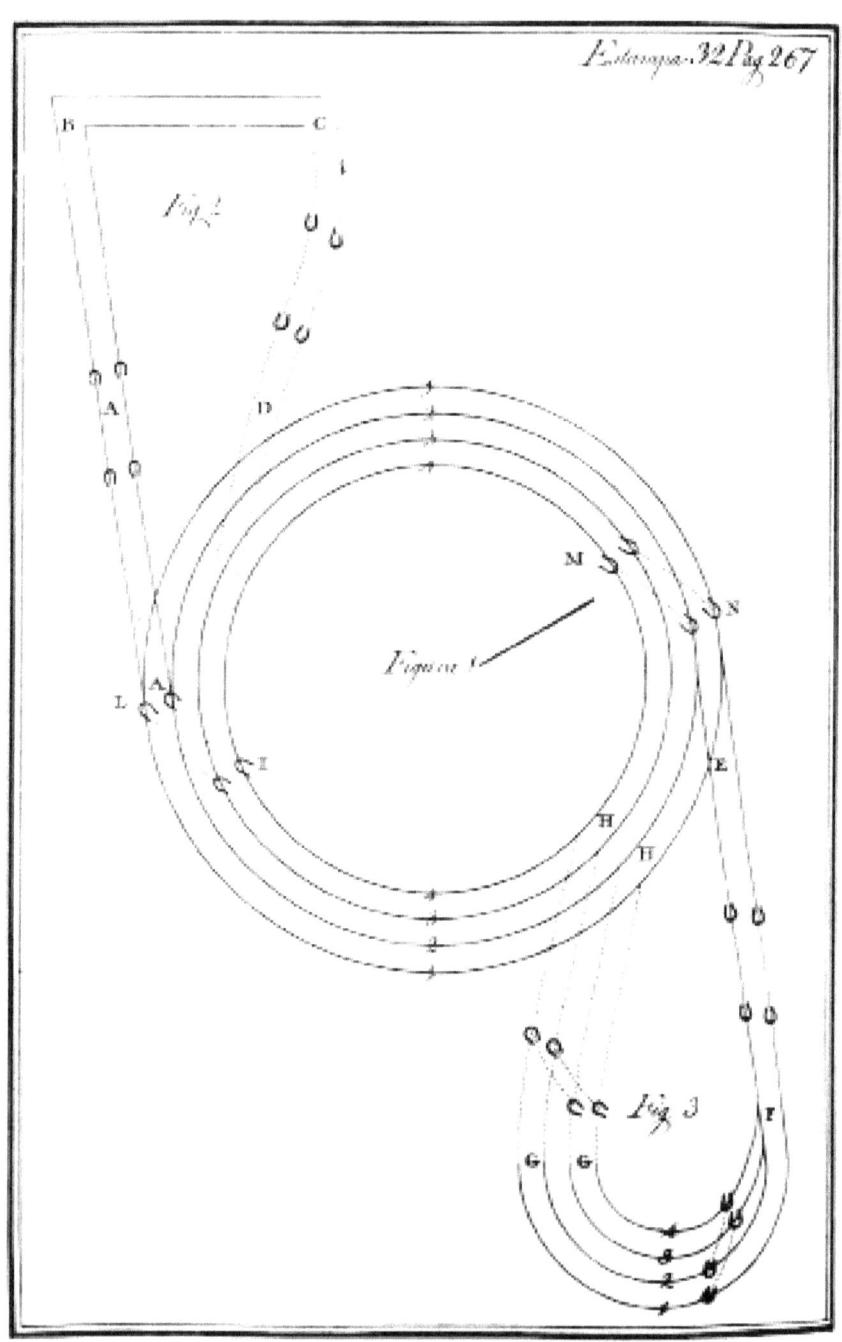

Haunches-in on the circle to the right and change of hand.

CHAPTER 1

THE OLD SCHOOL

LA GINETA, L'ESTRADIOTA, LA BRIDA

Portugal is the oldest country in Europe to maintain its borders. It became independent in 1140 following the victory by Dom Afonso Henriques, son of Henry, Comte de Bourgogne and Terese, daughter of King Léon, over the people of Mauitania: the Moors.

During 500 years of occupation, the Moors had spread their culture. By affiliating with the Portuguese people, they influenced the language, the architecture, the dress, the customs, the food... and the way to ride a horse!

They practiced and taught their own horsemanship: *la Gineta*. The Portuguese and Brazilian Encyclopedia defines *la Gineta*.as: "a system of horsemanship where the rider uses the stirrup leathers shorter than they are *a la Brida.*"[22]

It is believed that the stirrups only appeared about 340 A.D. The Romans, the Persians, the Celts, and the other peoples of antiquity knew neither saddle nor stirrups.

The Greek and Roman authors evoked a suspended strap or cord (*suppendanemen*) placed along the roads and used it to mount horses. They also used the lance[23] and made their horses kneel so as to mount them, just as one can still see it practiced by the bull keepers in the Portuguese countryside. It is quite probable that the Moors had already used saddles with leathers and stirrups, and rode Arab and Barb horses as well as their own crosses.

---

22 (French: *en Bride*, in a curb bit bridle, but with a sub-meaning of *frein*: brake, the style of riding used by the knights, practiced with very long stirrups)
23 (to vault)

Gineta

The jennet (*genet* comes from *Gineta*) means "rider–warrior." It finds its origin in the word "*zaneta*" which means "tribe of bold riders." It is also applied to a "horse of good breeding, fine conformation, light and well-trained." The "Z" is changed to "G" by the Portuguese, as in giraffe.

A rider's position is very different according to whether or not he uses stirrups. Historically, it is in this way that one can envision the succession of different types of riding in the Iberian Peninsula:

Estradiota: The rider is mounted without stirrups, the legs falling naturally. This was a "rider from the Levant (Middle East) composing the corps of light cavalry" as defined in the Portuguese and Brazilian Encyclopedia.

Gineta: The rider is mounted with short stirrup leathers. *Gineta* is practiced by the Iberian people and coexists with *la Brida*[24], the type of riding preferred by the riders of Northern Europe.

The bits in *Gineta* are "*tout entiers*" (entirely whole, one piece),

---

24 (more widely known as la Bride, see above)

which means that they are not articulated (not jointed) and the curb chain is replaced by a solid ring. The spurs are made of a pointed shaft like a little dagger. They touch the sides of the horse, always in the same place. The stirrups are in the form of an open box, pointed at the rear. This point, when it is long, frequently touches the flank of the horse, and can substitute for the spurs.

Iberian horses, supple and very light, allow the practice of a rapid horsemanship, at the gallop, with many turns, voltes, half-voltes, sudden halts, rein-backs, etc. This horsemanship corresponds to a particular form of fighting: that of the duel, as opposed to the horsemanship in formation practiced by those cavalries mounted on the large horses of the North.

The "crusaders" passed through Portugal in the course of their voyages to Jerusalem amd helped the first King of Portugal expel the Moors that had been present in Iberian lands since 710 A.D. From this association were born the exchanges between Brida and Gineta. A composite saddle appeared that they called the "bastard."

To manage the herds of cattle in the countryside while hunting or in combat, riders used the walk, the canter, or the gallop, never the trot. This is why *Eça de Queiroz* (Portuguese intellectual and writer) wrote: "It is certain that during the ancient life of wandering, *l'amour* (love) was, with battle and the gallop, an essential fact of Arab life." ***O Brida (La Bride)***: In the *Brida* or *Bride*[25] the rider rode with his stirrups so long that he was straight up sitting on his fork. The position is the same as that of the rider in the *Estradiota* position with the exception of the presence of stirrups.

Little by little *la Brida* evolved, and stirrup lengths became shorter.

The legs were placed so that the spurs could touch any part of the horse's belly, as well as his shoulders. By that time, *la Brida* already used the cavesson, the stick, and the long whip.

In combat, the riders in *la Brida* style attacked in straight line formation carrying all the weight of their tack and armor against the enemy line, or conversely formed large squares to envelop the enemy. The battle that opposed Louis XII (1462 – 1515) and his riders *a la Brida* to Ferdinand the Catholic (1452 – 1516) and his *écuyers a la Gineta* is a

---

25 Bridle

concrete example of the difference in the two systems.

On Louis XII's side, his heavy knights, dressed in metal breastplates, riding upright in their saddles, pressing heavily on their stirrups, moving slowly. On the other side, Ferdinand the Catholic's jennets, very light, their stirrup leathers very short, moving with stunning mobility, attacked the enemy in such a skillful fashion that victory smiled to the Castilians.

La Gineta is still practiced today in a nearly pure manner by Spanish riders in the countryside and in competition, under the name of *Doma vaquera*[26]. The Portuguese, skillful and naturally disposed to having tact, are champions in the tests of "Working Equitation," similar in a number of ways to the *Doma Vaquera*. *La Gineta* remains practical and necessary in the field, notably in the management of cattle, and of fighting bulls in particular.

La Brida influenced by *La Gineta*, evolved into the type of horsemanship that we use today in dressage.

ORIGINS AND DEVELOPMENT

"It was in the era of the renaissance of letters, science, and arts that dressage began to be taught with some method in Italy....As long as there were no schools, nor rational instruction, and as long as gentlemen boasted about not knowing how to read, or write, dressage would make no progress." (F. Musany, *Propos d'un Écuyer*, 1895, p. 28.)

Academies were founded in Naples, Rome, then in Tours, Bordeaux, Lyon. In France, the students learned not only dressage, but fencing, dance, the academic arts, and mathematics.

One can see that equestrian art held an important place in the education of the youth of higher rank. "Until the French Revolution, the position of *Écuyer* remained a title of nobility, and no one could take on the title of *Écuyer* if he was not the offspring of a father or grandfather ennobled in the military profession." (*Loc. cit.*, p. 29, note I.)

"One finds in the *Dictionnaire de l'Academie Française* (*éd. de* 1777), for the word Academy: ...said to be also a place where the nobility learned to ride horses and other exercises that were suitable." (*Loc. cit.*,

[26] Loosely: the traditional working riding tradition, originating from herding.

p.28, note I). If we add to this fact that the definition of the Academy of Music only comes later in the Dictionary, we have an idea of the importance of equestrian art in the education and culture of the *élites* of that time.

The Spanish occupation of the Kingdom of Naples was certainly not irrelevant to the development of horsemanship. The Andalusian horse must have given tone to its blossoming.

In the chapter on the *rassembler*, we explained how the Spanish horse, possessing within himself the style of *Haute École*, served as a model for horses of other breeds for which very collected airs were not so easy to perform. It became necessary to study the way to obtain these airs. One could say therefore that the modern science of horsemanship was born in Naples, and that it spread from there to the rest of Italy and Europe.

It was at the School of Naples that the French *écuyers*, La Broue, La Noue, and Pluvinel, received their instruction, and then brought the practices of the new equestrian science back to their country. Pluvinel was *Écuyer* to Louis XIII, for whom he wrote *Instruction du Roy* (1625) [*The Maneige Royal*, Xenophon Press 2010]) a true treatise, that introduced the dressage of Neopolitan *Haute École* into France. Expounding on the functioning of the Neopolitan procedures for the gentling of horses, he continued the simplification of the mouthpieces of bits begun by his master Pignatelli – mouthpieces about the effect of which he had said, "If bits by themselves had the miraculous property of making a horse's mouth and rendering him obedient, the rider and horse would be trained upon leaving a loriner's[27] shop." (L'Hotte, *Un Officier de Cavalerie*, 1905, p. 280.)

L'Instruction du Roy (*The Maneige Royal*, Xenophon Press 2010) went through many editions. With Pluvinel's book being the treatise most in vogue until the appearance of *L'École de Cavalerie* by La Guérinière (1733) [*École de Cavalerie, Part II*, Xenophon Press 1992], the rules of academic dressage were little by little dictated by France.

With La Guérinière we come to the apex of the Old School as a system. The means of domination becomes much less violent and the rider seated in a better position.

---

27 A person who made bits, spurs, and other small metal objects, *éperonier*

The line of illustrious *écuyers* from this era, during which the old way flourished, ended with La Bigne and the Viscount d'Abzac, the two most celebrated of the last *écuyers* from the Academy of Versailles that shut its doors in 1830.

D'Abzac appears to have been the personification of the kind of *écuyer* that the academy celebrated – the position and the delicacy of aids. The gentleness in the use of the means of domination made him a rider whose renown extended throughout all of Europe.

D'Abzac emigrated during the French revolution, and taught dressage in Hamburg. One day he met a German rider who having difficulty with his horse. He asked the rider, without making himself known, for permission to ride the horse. He succeeded in obtaining obedience so promptly that the rider exclaimed, "If you are not the devil, you are surely M. d'Abzac."

Of the Marquis de la Bigne, it is recounted that he won a bet to take an hour to cross the Place d'Armes[28] of the Palace of Versailles at the collected canter, using a silken cord as his only mouthpiece.[29]

Colonel d'Auvergne, who was certainly the greatest military rider of the XVIII century, taught a group of remarkable students at the Paris Military School, among them Boisdeffre, Bohan, and Chabannes, who published the principles and methods of their master's horsemanship. But against all logic, this remarkable military equitation at the end of the XVIII and beginning of the XIX century did not prevail at the new school at Saumur. In effect, M. de Chabannes, loyal successor of Colonel d'Auvergne, could not make his master's principles accepted there. He found himself in opposition to the *Écuyer en chef,* Cordier (1825 – 1833), defender, without a doubt abusively, of

---

28 parade square
29 M. d'Abzac and M. de La Bigne were both students of M. de Neuilly, *écuyer* to the Royal Manège. Two contemporaries of M. de Neuilly who were also *écuyers* at Versailles, Montfaucon de Rogles and Lubersac, went to the *Chevau-légers* (Light Horse) from the *Garde du Roy* (Royal Guard). They taught horsemanship at this company's *manège*. Lubersac was in function there as *Écuyer en chef* for twenty-one years (1744 – 1765). Both knew how to adapt academic dressage to the needs of the cavalry by simplifying its application. Colonel d'Auvergne, who had been their student at the *Chevau-légers*, was named *Écuyer en chef* at the *École Militaire de Paris*, of which the buildings and a *manège* still exist. He taught there for thirty-two years (1756 – 1788). (N.F.T.)

**Comte d'Aure about 1835, Museum of the Horse, Saumur.
"His solid and elegant silhouette [...]"-General Decarpentry.**

Versailles from which he had received only indirect training by way of the former staff members of the Royal *Manège*. Although M. de Chabannes' prestige far exceeded that of M. Cordier, the former was relieved of his duties after only two years of service (1825 – 1827).

In 1834, Marshal Soult, Minister of War[30], decided that the authority of *Écuyer en chef* should be given to someone whose prestige also came from a military rank. The first officer called on to command equestrian instruction would be Commandant Renaux, then Commandant Champet, a rider of somewhat too thin an equestrian experience to have left any trace. M. Rousselet (*Chef d'escadrons* retired) commanded the *Manège* in 1839 – 1840. Rousselet's equestrian refinement (finesse) was exemplary, but his discrete personality did not bring him to the forefront. He was content with thirty-four years of teaching of which twenty-three after 1825, were at the School of Saumur under the authority of the *Écuyers en chef* mentioned above, then under the command of Novital (1841 – 1846), and finally under Comte D'Aure (1847 – 1855). When he retired, Marshal Soult, refused to reverse his decision to not name any more civilian *écuyers* to Saumur. The Duc de Nemours, former student

30 Marshal Soult commanded the second French invasion of Portugal in 1809.

of Comte d'Aure, succeeded in placing his master at the head of the *Manège*.

D'Aure had been the most renowned of the students of d'Abzac, and then, at the death of d'Abzac in 1827, became his successor, and had held that post until the definite closure of the Academy of Versailles in 1830. He was then thirty-one years old. The still young Viscount manifested his preference for outdoor equitation that had started to become the leading fashion of the time. D'Aure professed his taste for horses destined to the hunt, flat racing, and the steeplechase. His reputation came to him more by his remarkable gift for improvisation, and from his solid seat and elegant silhouette that allowed him to highlight the natural qualities of the horse, than from a special skill in the work of *Haute École*.

While everyone hoped that d'Aure would continue the traditions of the Academy of Versailles, the great rider let himself go to exploits that demonstrated his exceptional seat, riding some difficult young horses at the fairgrounds of Normandy and the Thoroughbreds of Lord Seymour – at that time the arbiter of elegance in Paris. As a result *Haute École* was a game left a bit to the side.

Le Cerf, the horse that d'Aure had trained at Versailles under the direction of d'Abzac, served as his "living *écuyer* certificate." It was not as a high school *écuyer*, in all that it demands of method and reflection, that Comte d'Aure made his reputation, but rather, in the ease and brilliance with which he rode a trained horse.

D'Aure often saved himself by lucky improvisation. He also committed grave faults. This was the case in the course of a celebrated meeting that he had in his *manège* with Baucher. While presenting a mare that he wanted to sell to Baucher, he forced her to change lead at the canter without her having been prepared. After having demonstrated a great deal of ill will, the mare ended up by passing through the door of the stable three times straight up on her hind legs, and even d'Aure's terrible attacks with the spurs did not succeed in getting her to submit.

Baucher murmured to his student, Maxine Gaussen, who was present at the encounter, "It is a massacre!"

During a visit to Saumur, General de Brack invited d'Aure alone to ride the best-trained horse in the school: *Sans pareil*, son of Commandant Rousselet's celebrated *Sans pareil*. D'Aure, barely in the

Le Cerf, trained and ridden by Comte d'Aure. Treaty of equitation. "Comte d'Aure's method was completely personal unto himself."
General Decarpentry.

saddle, went to the whip, exciting the horse to demonstrate his power of domination and boldness.

It is too bad that this man, so exceptionally gifted, preferred to show his audacity rather than his tact. He had a great gift for tact, evidenced by the way he rode the same horse the next day. The harmony between rider and horse astounded all those in attendance.

It was a great loss for the Old School that after the closure of the

Partisan, trained and ridden by François Baucher; at the piaffe in 1840 – First Manner

Academy of Versailles, this *écuyer* with the greatest of reputations did not continue its traditions. If it had been so, Baucher, who had qualified d'Aure as a "Centaur," would have found a true equestrian rival. But this rivalry took only the form of controversy that was set up between each master's own disciples and not the form of a serious argument.

After d'Aure resigned from Saumur in 1855 to take the directorship of the Imperial Stables, Commandant Guérin, a member of the Cadre Noir for fourteen years, became *Écuyer en Chef* for eight years. During the duration of his command, Commandant Guérin, now *Capitaine-Écuyer,* authored a work for use by instructors, *École du Cavalier au Manège* (1851) [School of the *Manège* Rider], while he was. He then published in 1860 *Dressage du Cheval de Guerre* (Training of the War Horse), the title of which is without equivocation and which nevertheless is in line with Baucherist principles.

Commandant L'Hotte, the eulogist of Baucher, successor to Guérin as *Écuyer en Chef* used all the methods that hehad taken from Baucher for the dressage of his personal horses. Then L'Hotte re-established d'Aurist training at Saumur. Later, as commanding General of the School, he confirmed his prohibition of Baucherism "in his own writing in the purest d'Aurist orthodoxy: The Training of Horses Regulations of 1876 for the Cavalry." (Decarpentry, *Baucher et son École*, 1948, p. 132.*Baucher and his School,* Xenophon Press 2011)

In spite of renewed instruction "tainted by Baucherism," like that of Commandant Dutilh, *Écuyer en Chef* in 1875 – 1876, d'Aurism has prevailed at the Cavalry School. General Decarpentry had reason to write, "Comte d'Aure was the founder of the military equitation practiced in France for a century....For certain persons, Comte d'Aure maintained the tenuous connection that united the School at Saumur to that of Versailles. Nothing could be less accurate....Comte d'Aure's method was completely personal and it deviates from those of Versailles as much by its principles as by its practice." (Decarpentry, *Les Maîtres Écuyers du Manège de Saumur*, 1954, p. 69.)

ORGANIZATION

We have already spoken about the origins of the horsemanship of the Old School and the celebrity of its *écuyer*s. Now let us review the way that it was organized across the centuries in France (from René Bacharach, *L'Année Hippique*, 1961 – 1962).

There had already been noted by the VI century a *Comes stabuli*, or Count of the Stables. We run into it under the name *Connestable* and later *Connétable* (Constable). Charged at first with the management of the royal stables, he later became the commander of the mounted troop, and then the commanding officer of all of the army.

The etymology of the word *écuyer* (equerry, now an honorific title for a British Royal Aide-de-Camp) is the Latin word *scutarius* (shield-maker) – the *écuyer* is the gentleman who accompanied the knight and "*porte l'écu*" (carried the shield). From the beginning of the Middle Ages, the kings of France surrounded themselves with *écuyers*. The functions of some were connected to the handling of horses – the one in charge being *Écuyer du Corps* (equerry of the body), close to the royal person to defend him as needed – and the function of the others concern the government of the stables – the one in charge being *Écuyer du Tynel* (the name of the building), later *Écuyer du Séjour* (the location of the stables).

From the end of the XIII century to the beginning of the XV century, these functions were conjoined and the one in charge was called *Premier Écuyer du Corps et Grand Maître de l'Écurie* (First Equerry of the Body and Grand Master of the Stable).

In 1441, Charles VII created the office of *Grand Écuyer* for Jean Poton de Xaintrailles, Companion-in-Arms to La Hire and to Jeanne d'Arc.

This office would be maintained without interruption until 1792. It reappeared with Napoleon I, and then was abolished in 1870.

The *Grand Écuyer de France* (*Monsieur le Grand*) one of the primary dignitaries of the Kingdom, was the superintendent of the two "*Écuries du Roi*" (King's Stables), the Grande (the "big stable" for saddle horses) and the Petite (the "small stable" for harness horses), with the personnel attached to them, the *Haras Royal* (Royal Stud), the *Maison des Pages* (House of the Pages, a sort of cadet corps of student officers), and the Equestrian Academies in Paris and the provinces. For an idea of the importance of the Royal Stables in France, let us say that under Louis XIV, the *Grand Écurie* accounted for 180 horses, under Louis XV, 250, and under Louis XVI, 300. By that time there were 200 in the *Petite Écurie*. But taking count of the horses for hunting, for couriers, and for various kinds of transport, the *Maison du Roi* (King's Household) presented an effective strength of more than 4000 horses.

All of the expenses, ordinary and extraordinary, of the stables were authorized by the *Grand Écuyer* who named all the officers, except the *Premier Écuyer de la Petite Écurie* (*Monsieur le Premier*, Sir "the first", First *Écuyer* of the Small Stable) who was appointed directly by the King. Over two centuries, from Henri IV to Louis XVI, the post remained hereditary, within the House of the Princes of Lorraine. Such continuity in the organization and supervision of French civilian horsemanship allowed its excellent development.

In order to comprehend the importance of the *écuyers* of the *Grand Écurie du Roi* (the trainers of the saddle horses of Versailles), it is necessary to understand their formation. Access to the *Grand Écurie* for equestrian training and education was the privilege of young gentlemen who could attest to at least four generations of military nobility.

Armed with their accredited certificates of genealogy, the applicants had to address their request for admission as a page in the *Grand Écurie* to Monsieur le Grand, usually at fifteen years of age. This primary instruction theoretically lasted for three years. Besides their instruction in equitation, the pages received an excellent general education. When they left the *Grande Écurie*, the greater part of them had gained a military promotion to Cavalry Officer.

Louis XV, the well-loved

A very small number of Pages among those who rode the best could, on their request addressed to the *Grand Écuyer*, be named *Éleves Écuyers* (Student *Écuyers*). Their instruction lasted three or four years. The best of the *Éleves Écuyers* could then be named *Écuyers Cavalcadours*. Their functions consisted of accompanying the King in his outings on horseback, or in a carriage, and of instructing the Pages and training the young horses.

Of the *Écuyers Cavalcadours*, only the most skillful could become *Écuyers Ordinaires*. These were three or four in number. They trained the horses and taught the Pages. They directed the equestrian education in the *Grand Écurie*.

After the end of the XVI century, the Royal Academies of Horsemanship, authorized by Monsieur le Grand, were created in Paris and in the provinces. At first, the teachers of horsemanship came from the *Grand Écurie*, and later were trained in the Academies themselves. They would nevertheless be nominated exclusively by the *Grand Écuyer*

Baucher on Buridan at the piaffe.

**Capitaine, trained and ridden by François Baucher in 1840.
Lengthened trot in descent of the hand.
Rapid stop from the gallop, the horse light, the haunches well under.**

who would confer on them the title of *Écuyer du Roi* (King's Écuyer).

The Royal Academies (ten in Paris, and seventeen of some importance in the provinces) turned out riders of renown, but the academies hardly knew prosperity. They were gravely hit by the creation of the Military School by Louis XV, where free instruction was furnished to five hundred poor gentlemen. The Constituent Assembly (during the French Revolution) shut down The Royal Academies.

Various military and regimental schools of horsemanship were founded during the second half of the XVIII Century and in the beginning of the XIX Century. Many of them attained celebrity. Eventually the teaching of military horsemanship was almost entirely centralized in Saumur after 1825. We have already described its early history.

THE GOAL

The goal of Old School horsemanship was to bring the horse into a balance that allowed him to calmly execute the High School airs (passage, piaffer, levade, "terre-a-terre") and the airs above the ground (mezair, courbette, ballotade and capriole).

This balance supposes an extreme degree of collection of the horse on the haunches. Such a balance is facilitated by the use of a horse with a conformation comparable to that of Iberian horses. These horses were the most esteemed of the School Horses. But their exportation was forbidden by Spain in the XVIII Century. Other horses of heavier weight and less fine temperament were used, such as Neapolitan horses, those of the Navarrine breed, Limousine, (with Spanish genetic influence) etc. As a testimony to the favor enjoyed by the Andalusian horse, let us cite the fact that in the dowry that Catarina de Bragança brought to England for her marriage to Charles II, there were twelve Portuguese mares. We should also recall that Louis XIII's horse, Bonito, trained by Pluvinel, and Louis XV's horse, Florido, trained by Nestier both had names that attest to their peninsular origin.

THE METHOD

"The Low School of the old masters was composed of an ensemble of exercises necessary and sufficient to render the horse

**Laruns, trained and ridden by then Colonel L'Hotte, around 1866.
"[...] and in certain cases, inside of the vertical." - Diogo de Bragança**

sure and comfortable in his ordinary use in service under saddle. The horse's gymnastics, particularly oriented toward this goal , constituted nonetheless an important and efficient element in directing him toward the special education required by High School, but the Low School did not pretend to lead the horse there directly, and only envisioned that goal as an eventuality necessitating a complement of preparation, notably as it concerned the *rassembler*, which it sought by use of the pillars." (Decarpentry, *L'Essentiel de la Méthode de Haute École de Raabe*. 1957 p. 93.)

Thus, the Low School of the Old Masters was followed by work in the pillars and only afterward was High School started. Later, Baucherism did not have any use for the pillars as a preparatory technique to academic dressage.

LA GUÉRINIÈRE'S PROGRESSION

For the dressage of the horse

At first, walk and shoulder-in at the walk, change of hand on the straight, croup to the wall on both hands, *doubler* (ninety degree turn off the wall, across the school, ninety degree turn on the wall on the same hand) down the length of the school at the walk. Energetic trot on a single track, same trot in a doubler length of the school without croup to the wall. Come back to shoulder-in at the walk, then to croup to the wall, and finish by a doubler down the length of the school.

The pillars (invention attributed to Pluvinel) are in the first place only used to teach the horse to cadence himself in place, without advancing, nor backing, nor traversing himself, and not right away to make the horse lift the forehand.

After having described the first lessons in the pillars, in which the horse placed in the middle of the ropes that attach the cavesson to the pillars, must mobilize his croup from one side to the other, and step forward according to the indications from the *écuyer*, La Guérinière said that one should make the horse kick, especially those horses that have little mobility of their croup, because this movement gymnasticizes the hocks, supples the haunches, gives agility to the hindquarters, etc. "The experience makes us see," wrote this author, "that a horse that has never been made to kick has stiff haunches, and in movement, trails them

Iran, trained and ridden by Captain de Saint-Phalle
In 1907. Passage.
A little open, but harmonious and light.

Rampart, trained and ridden By Colonel Wattel. Passage.
Elegance, sobriety, energy, lightness.
As Écuyer en Chef at the Saumur School, Colonel Wattel honored the
Baucherist formula: "Hand without leg, leg without hand."

behind." (*École de Cavalerie, éd. in octavo*, 1754, p. 213. [*School of Horsemanship Part II*, Xenophon Press 1992])

It is only after the horse piaffes calmly in the pillars that one begins to make the forehand lift to prepare the "parade"[31] and the passage.

For the education of the rider

Six months at the trot without stirrups, correct the position in the pillars, and then ride the horse in the demi-courbette, the courbette, the croupade, the ballotade, and finally the capriole.

Action of the hand according to La Guérinière: "The hand must always begin the first effect and the legs must accompany this movement; because it is a general principle that in all the airs, both natural and artificial, the head and shoulders of the horse must move first; and as the horse has four principal movements, which are to go forward, to go back, to go to the right, and to go to the left, the bridle hand must also produce four effects, which are, to give the hand, to resist with the hand, to turn the hand to the right, and to turn the hand to the left." (*Loc. cit.*, p. 160.)

In describing the way to work with the reins in the left hand, La Guérinière puts the rider on guard against an error that it is only too easy to commit. It is necessary, when one acts with the right hand on the right rein "to bend the horse to the right, that the feeling of the outside rein remain in the left hand, so that the bend comes from the withers and not from the end of the nose, an ugly movement....In a way that when one works a horse to the right, it does not suffice to shorten the right rein to bend him, one is often obliged to use the right rein by taking it with the little finger of the right hand, which functions like the little finger of the left hand when one works to the left." (*Loc. cit.* p. 162.)

According to the action of the hand one can give the horse an arching bend or the *demi-pli*[32] in which the horse "looks into his volte with only one eye." This latter degree of incurvation (a curvature that turns inward) was preferred by La Guérinière.

---

31 (halt from the collected canter)
32 (Literally: "partial bend." Inside positioning of the head and neck.)

THE TROT AS THE BASIC GAIT OF DRESSAGE

Salomon de la Broue wrote that "a well-trained horse is one that has suppleness, obedience, and correctness." La Guérinière cited him and added: "The first of these qualities is acquired only by the trot. That is the general sentiment of all the learned *écuyers*, the old and the modern, and if among the modern, some have wanted, without any foundation, to reject the trot, seeking in a little collected walk this primary suppleness and liberty, they are in the wrong, because one can only give these qualities to a horse by putting into strong movement all the springs of his machine." (*Loc. cit.*, p. 176.) It seems in effect that with this stylization of the walk, nature goes to sleep, obedience becomes sluggish and tardy, and in this condition one is far from the true brilliance that adorns a well-trained horse. It is by the trot that the horse becomes light without spoiling the mouth, that his legs are freed, because in this action, which is the most elevated of the natural gaits. The body of the horse takes an equal weight on the two legs of a diagonal which gives the other two that are in the air the ability to lift, to suspend, and to extend, and by consequence to acquire a superior degree of suppleness.

"The trot is then, without contradiction, the base of all lessons for rendering a horse dexterous and obedient." (*Loc. cit.*, p. 176.)

GENERAL ACTIONS

In the *general actions*, equestrian gymnastics are obtained by aids that act on the whole body of the horse.

The principal exercises used by the Old School were not addressed just to one part of the horse, for example the jaw, or the croup; they acted on the whole horse to make him move in the direction and position requested by the aids.

The most commonly used *general actions* were the work in the pillars (criticized by the Duke of Newcastle), the halt, the half-halt, and the most important of all, the shoulder-in.

According to La Guérinière, the halt consists of an effect produced by the action of the hand that supports the forehand of the horse, at the same time he is brought to engage his hindquarters by a delicate effect of the rider's legs so that the horse halts in balance on

**Jiorno, trained and ridden by Diogo de Bragança.
Trot with good impulsion in descent of the hand.**

his haunches. In the half-halt, the hand, close to the body and acting upwards, holds the horse without at any moment halting him completely, but supporting the forehand, whether it is when the horse leans on the bit, or when one wants the *ramener*, or the *rassembler*.

We have already mentioned the pillars. Let us see how La Guérinière arrived at the formula for the shoulder-in that he considered the alpha and omega of gymnastic exercises given to the horse.

Monsieur de la Broue found that for gymnasticising the shoulders, the volte is certainly an excellent means, but few physical constitutions could support prolonged work on the circle. The majority of horses would finish by contracting instead of suppling the shoulders. For this reason, instead of work on the circle, he preferred work on the square.

The Duke of Newcastle practiced work on the circle with the head to the inside and the croup to the outside. And while recognizing that this exercise (another general action) put the horse on the shoulders and made him lean on the bit, Newcastle thought that the shoulders could be suppled if the inside hind advanced well under the body and approached the outside hind.

Piaffer.
The result of work in lightness *(légèreté.)*

It is in account of this last observation of Newcastle, confirmed by the experience "that the circle is not the correct means of perfectly suppling the shoulders, because a thing constrained and loaded by its own weight cannot be light," (*Loc. cit.*, p. 197.) that La Guérinière discovered the lesson of the shoulder-in.

In this exercise, the rider brings the horse's shoulders to the inside of the school track by bending him toward the hand to which he is travelling. This way the horse goes on two tracks, the haunches close to the wall and the shoulders detached from the wall in the neighborhood of "a foot and a half or two" bent away from the direction in which he is moving.

With this work (shoulder-in on the wall) the quality that Newcastle attributed to the circle, the freedom of the shoulders is developed, because the inside hind comes under the weight and steps in front of (but not beyond) the outside hind, thus avoiding the inconvenience mentioned by the same author, knowing that the circle puts the horse on the shoulders when the inside hind does not advance well under the body.

The movement of the hind legs in the shoulder-in is in effect favorable to the lowering of the haunches, a disposition that prepares for the *rassembler*. Outside of these advantages, the shoulder-in contributes to a good placement of the neck and head, and habituates the croup to move under the action of the rider's legs.

THE OLD SCHOOL *RASSEMBLER*

By analyzing the means employed (the pillars, the trot, the shoulder-in...), one can see that the Old School *rassembler* was a matter of making the horse in training acquire, little by little, the faculty to shift the major part of his weight on to the hindquarters, to approach the concept that was expressed later as a "horse powerful in the haunches and gallant in the mouth."

The Old School sought, at the three gaits, the type of *rassembler* comprising the complete *ramener*, the bending of the haunches and the lateral placement of the head toward the hand on which the horse was working. It resulted in a great facility for the practice of elevated airs and School jumps whiche resulted in some difficulty in executing sequence changes of lead and for the pirouette with distinctly separated beats of the canter.

The *ramener*, an element of the *rassembler*, was obtained by the progressive engagement of the hind legs under the body, and the mounted rider did not hesitate, in order to preserve it, to employ powerful bits and spurs with pointed rowels, while the rider working in hand from the ground used the cavesson, the "dumb jockey[33]," the pillars, and the surcingle with various side-reins.

LA GUÉRINIÈRE'S "SQUARE"

The horse in the *rassembler* showed the degree of balance achieved in his training by working on a square of small dimensions, passaging on the sides, and piaffing in the corners. The *terre à terre*[34] is transformed into quarter pirouettes or into quarter reverse pirouettes in the corners. They worked on the square this way to confirm the horse to the aids, to determine the bend to give the horse in the voltes (always on two tracks in the old terminology), and to refine the dressage of an already advanced horse. On one square they exercised in ordinary voltes, on another square the reverse voltes. On the first, the horse moved with the hindquarters on the sides of the squares so that the forehand moved on parallel tracks outside of the square. In the corners, the hind legs moved in place so that the shoulders described a quarter of a circle. This is what the French called "embracing the volte." They practiced the contrary on the reverse voltes, that is to say that the forehand moves on the sides of the square, the hindquarters travelling on an outside track parallel to the sides of the square and in the corners, the forelegs move in place while the croup describes a quarter of a circle on the outside.

THE OLD SCHOOL AIRS

One must carefully distinguish the Old School airs from what we see today. The old concept was completely different because the horse had a completely different conformation.

The Old School passage derived from piaffe (in Germany, the *écuyers* came to piaffe out of the rein-back while progressively sitting the horse down).

The pirouette did not show separated beats of the canter. They required that the horse turn around the inside hind leg making a pivot.

[33] A device used to accustom an untrained horse to a bridle and saddle, attached to the horse where the saddle would be fastened.
[34] A very collected canter in two beats and often on two tracks, used to prepare the airs.

**Jiorno, trained and ridden by Diogo de Bragança.
Passage. Cadence, with a very light contact on the bit.**

Since the final goal was to get to the elevated airs and School jumps, we do not have a means of comparison because the School jumps are hardly practiced today, except at the School in Vienna. However it is interesting to recall that Captain Raabe advocated the practice of the courbette to get to the pirouette. But let us note that the description of the courbette by Raabe (Decarpentry, *L'Essentiel de la Méthode de Haute École de Raabe*, 1957, p. 170) is different from the courbette of the Old School, and from the interpretation at the Vienna School. It amounts in fact to a *mézair* (demi-air or demi-courbette, between a terre à terre and courbette).

The Old School *écuyers* did not practice the changes of lead at the canter as one sees today. Actually, today they are executed *"en l'air"* ("in the air"), that is to say without an intermediate beat, while in the old manner, they were made in two beats – the horse marking a very slight time at halt before retaking the canter on the other lead. It is what we call execution *"de ferme à ferme"*[35]. (Description by General Decarpentry, *Équitation Academique*, 1949, p. 240) Baucher attributed another meaning to this expression. He wrote in his *Dictionnaire*: "They call working *ferme à ferme*, to summon the horse to perform without moving out of place, as in piaffe."

To come back to the *mézair*, as in Raabe's practice in the preparation of the pirouette, let us recall Baucher's definition, in his *Dictionnaire raisonné d'Équitation* (1833), "The mézair is a series of jumps forward, where the forelegs are lifted from the ground less than in the courbette; also, the horse makes the jumps in a more lively succession."

In any event, the practice of very collected canter (*galop rassemblé*) in the Old School was pushed up to the point where the horse raised the forehand appreciably. In effect, after having examined the ordinary three beat canter, such as we observe currently, La Guérinière wrote (*École de Cavalerie*, pp. 139 – 140 [*School of Horsemanship Part II*, Xenophon Press 1992]), "But when the horse has his *ressorts* (springs, joints) flexible and the movement of the haunches *tride*[36], he makes four beats that are made in the following order: When he canters to the right for example, the left hind foot touches the ground first, the right hind is the second beat, immediately after that the left fore marks the third beat, and finally the right fore, which is the most advanced of them all, marks the fourth and last; which makes then 1, 2, 3, and 4, and forms the true cadence of a good canter..." He also called it *gallopade* or school canter (*galop de manège*), and specifies that this is "a united canter, well gathered, collected in front and prompt in the haunches; that is to say a canter that does not trail behind, and that produces, by the equality of the *ressorts* (springs, joints) of the horse, that beautiful cadence that charms the spectators as much as it pleases the rider." (*Loc. cit.,* p. 146.)

---

35 From firm ground to firm ground.
36 Lively, quick, short and ready

THE OLD SCHOOL OF PORTUGAL

With the publication of the work of King Dom Duarte, *Livro da Ensinança de Bem Cavalgar Toda Sela* – the manuscript of which is in the National Library in Paris (Bacarach has arrived at the conclusion that the date of Duarte's work is 1434) [*The Royal Book of Horsemanship, Jousting and Knightly Combat*, "The Art of Riding on Every Saddle," The Chivalry Bookshelf, Highland Village, Texas. Antonio Franco Preto, the English translator, put the date at 1438,] There appeared the first of the great books on dressage written by Portuguese authors. French historians considered the work of Frederico Grisone (1550) the first known treatise on dressage after that of Xenophon – which preceded it by nearly twenty centuries. Yet Duarte's work preceded Grisone's by one hundred and sixteen years. It is an entirely original book. The author does not speak of what he has heard, but of what he has learned from great practice, the fruit of his own experience and reflection.

Among the most important Portuguese works on dressage, we must cite *Arte de Cavalaria da Gineta e Estradiota..* (The Art of Cavalry a la Gineta and Estradiota) by Galvão de Andrade (1678), *Instrução da Cavalaria de Brida* (The Instruction of the Cavalry in the "a la Brida" style) by Antonio Pereyra Rego (1679), and Manoel Carlos de Andrade's book *Luz da Liberal et Nobre Arte da Cavallaria* (Light of the Liberal and Noble Art of the Cavalry, 1790) in which de Andrade describes the methods put into practice by D. Pedro de Alcantara e Menezes, general of cavalry and *écuyer*, Marquis of Marialva, who gave his prestige to the Royal *Manège* of Belem (Lisbon) as well as to the Haras Real d'Alter do Chão (Royal Stud at Alter do Chão).

Here is what Manoel Carlos de Andrade said about the celebrated Marquis: "He works no matter what horse, whether on the straight, or croup to the pillar (around a single post), or head to the wall, or shoulders to the center (around a single post), or in all the figures of the *manège* that are made at the walk, at the trot, at the canter, in *terre-à-terre* and in the elevated airs with a perfection that I have not yet seen in any other rider. Every action of his body, of his hands, and of his legs is so appropriate and so in accordance, be it to aid, or be it to chastise the horse, that the animal obeys him to the limits of his capabilities."

"He devotes himself to the noble art of riding with such care and persistence that, at more than seventy-six years of age, he directs the training (in the school) every day, working many horses and colts with as much ease and vivacity as if he were still a young man, to the confusion of those men who let themselves go to the most sinful laziness...."

"There are some riders who ride well the horses that are trained by others, and there are riders who possess the gift, the knowledge, and the talent to set up, bring along, and train horses from the first principles of the Art, and in proceeding with method, all the way to the most complete education in all the lessons that they must receive. Among the best teachers, General D. Pedro de Alcantara e Menezes was the one that possessed the gift, the knowledge, and the talent nearest to perfection."

LUZ DA L'ARTE LIBERA NOBRE DA CAVALARIA

(UNDERSTANDING *THE LIBERAL AND NOBLE ART OF CAVALRY*)

(*DIE EDLE KUNST DES REITENS,* Olms 2006)

In his book published in 1790, Manoel Carlos de Andrade demonstrates his knowledge of the best treatises. It builds on the instruction recommended by the masters that preceded him, and derives the most judicious application of those instructions. One should be aware notably of the application that Andrade makes of La Broue's work on the square, Newcastle's work on the circle, and La Guérinière's shoulder-in.

Andrade recommends (p. 193) beginning the horse's work on the circle. He gives us precious information on the shoulder-in (p. 194): "Horses that are difficult to turn, on one hand or the other, should not be worked in the lesson of the shoulder-in so that they do not take advantage of the aid of the outside hand to practice their defense. Instead, they should be worked on the longe line on the circle, then on straight lines the whole length of the wall and on lines of the square, until abandoning their faults, thus allowing themselves to be conquered and dominated."

"The lesson of the shoulder-in, if the horse is not reluctant to move forward, is very profitable. It is taken from the lessons on the circle on two and four tracks, and has the same goal as the lessons on the circle, because it supples the shoulder and the forelegs well, and prepares well for the demi-haunches-in."

"The shoulders of the horse cannot be placed to the inside, in this lesson, without the horse taking on a demi-haunches-in, and the inside hind, engaging under the body, coming in on the line of the outside fore;

The Marquis de Marialva at the capriole. Andrade 1790.

Of the School jumps, Dupaty de Clam wrote In 1776, "The Old Masters would love this kind of schooling; Today it is quite neglected in France."

so the horse is brought to not only lower the inside haunch, but to bend the hock and the fetlock in taking on a demi-haunches-in."

The Duke of Newcastle criticized the use of the pillars, the invention of which is attributed to Pluvinel. The invention that Newcastle advocated is that of the lateral effect of additional reins on the cavesson, attached to the pommel of the saddle, passing through a lateral ring on the nose band of the cavesson, and coming back to the rider's hand.

Manoel Carlos de Andrade counseled the use of either this lateral rein, or the pillars, which were also used by La Guérinière.

Luz da Liberal e Nobre Arte da Cavalaria is a treatise on horsemanship that is equal to the best of the era, perhaps even of a superior quality. Moreover, the engravings that illustrate it are admirable from an equestrian point of view. One could consider those showing us the Marquis de Marialva to be models of correctness.

If we compare the engravings found in the important works on the old horsemanship published in France and Portugal, we notice that, as it concerns position, La Guérinière's riders wore their stirrups very long – the upper body is well behind the vertical, but the rider's back is very arched. It certainly resulted in a beautiful position, but one that must have made difficult the adherence of the rider's legs to the body of the horse, especially in certain airs practiced at the canter. In Manoel Carlos de Andrade's book we see riders well seated, but more bent in the knee, which allows them a constant communication with their mount. According to our thinking, some engravings that represent the Marquis de Marialva show us an ideal position that could genuinely serve as a model.

THE ART OF MARIALVA

Technical analysis of Manoel Carlos de Andrade's book demonstrates the exceptional talent of the Marquis de Marialva. It is regrettable to hear today people speaking of "a new Marialva" or of "Marialvism" when these terms are applied to persons or deeds that have nothing to do with the Noble Art...

The expression "*Arte de Marialva*" that one hears so often in Portugal describes an ensemble of airs and rules that were put into practice over the course of the XVIII century and that the Marquis of that time made prominent. Those are different from the fantasies which many riders practice, and that are commonly called "*Marialvades*," or from the art of fighting bulls from horseback, in which the rider can, in fact, use some of the rules of the art of Marialva to dominate his mount. But he is brought to distance himself from many of them in order to attain the goal that he seeks.

Essentially, the Marquis de Marialva, whose art inspired Manoel Carlos de Andrade, was an exceptional executor of the most refined school horsemanship of his era, in the style instituted by the French *écuyers*, and comparison with the greatest of them would not be unfavorable to him.

In summary, he was a Portuguese *écuyer* of the French School. One can judge this not only by his applications of the French masters' methods, but even by the style of his clothes (which had separately been introduced into the Portuguese Court) and by his horses' tack, the saddles often qualified as "Portuguese" being none other than reproductions of "*selles à piquer, à la royale,* or *à la demi-royale.*"[37] Thus, in the XVIII century, the Portuguese School was inspired by French dressage.

EXAMINATION OF OLD SCHOOL EQUITATION

The dressage of Old School equitation had as a goal the practice of elevated airs and School jumps. We will analyze the means employed, and we will examine whether they were the most appropriate to the results that they proposed to attain.

Outside of the exercises of the low school, to prepare the horses for the School jumps, the *écuyers* of the XVIII century used a number of accessories: pillars, cavessons, fixed side reins, bits with powerful action and often even brutal effect.

The piaffe was considered more as an excellent preparation for the School jumps than as an air, properly said.

It must not be forgotten that the horsemanship of which we speak here – that of the XVIII century – was a development, a refinement of the horsemanship of war from preceding centuries. It's primary goal was to train for individual combat on horseback, and little by little, the quality that the warrior sought in a trained horse was, more than his speed, his facility in turning in any direction, and in leaping forward.

One must not criticize lightly this old horsemanship. It had its purpose. It used the means permitted to attain its goals. It was a practical and rational horsemanship, deserving consideration.

Today those who want to practice the School jumps must call upon Old School horsemanship. The modern form given to the airs above the ground by the School at Saumur appear to me to leave much to be desired. It has lost the beauty that the *rassembler* gave to the old airs above the ground, airs of which we can fortunately see executed by the horses at the Spanish Riding School of Vienna. It is true that these horses are bred and specially selected. But if their temperament and conformation allow their *écuyers* to bring them to the elevated airs, they do it according to the old concept of airs above the ground.

---

[37] See Commandant Licart, *Évolutions Équestres à travers les ages*, Olivier Perrin Éditeur, Paris, 1963 for pictures.

It is not without reason that Baucher reproached the Old School for having worked against the resistances of the horse. Even if it brought its horses up to the airs above the ground, it must not be forgotten that very few horses had the constitution to enable the execution of those airs.

It would be interesting to know if, in the Old School, lightness was considered the "touchstone of higher dressage" as it was after Baucher.

We know that the principal manifestations of lightness are the relaxation of the jaw and the mobility of the haunches. Baucher, using the methods that he discovered, succeeded in obtaining total lightness, but he particularly insisted on lightness of the jaw, proving that it is just as much the cause as the effect of general flexibility, while the Old School was preoccupied principally with the lightness of the haunches.

Must the lightness in the mouth, the natural consequence of the maximum engagement of the hindquarters in the *rassembler* of the Old School, be partially avoided in the elevated airs with the horse taking a definite contact (*appui*) on the hand? I think not, as the engravings from the period show. Firm contact (*appui*) can be noticed today in the exhibitions given by the Spanish Riding School of Vienna. (It is possible to get an idea of the degree of contact (*appui*) by observing the pronounced tightness of the horses' nose bands, or, in certain photographs, the opening of their mouths.)

One could ask if, in the Old School, there was not a contradiction between the impulsion that the riders demanded and the posture of *rassembler* that they gave to their horses.

If they wanted impulsion, why surcharge the croup and hocks, the horse's instruments of propulsion?

I believe that one can find the answer in the fact that they demanded great mobility, which can be obtained only from a horse working on a short base of support, that is, from a horse in *rassembler*.

If the sitting position is favorable to lateral mobility, it still brakes the impulsion, the conservation of which was in consequence the dominant preoccupation of the rider who gave his horse the position of "a cat about to jump onto a table," as was said by the Baucherists criticizing the *écuyers* from the School of Versailles. This preoccupation was necessary. The idea was to not let the impulsion "cool down" so that the horse would not have a tendency to remain on the haunches, thus making the transition from *rassembler* to a more horizontal balance difficult. Fortunately, as remarked Maxime Gaussen, the Old School *rassembler* disposed the flexors of the neck in relation with those of the croup so harmoniously that this posture presents no obstacle to forward movement.

One can read this observation next to the one of General Decarpentry concerning the trot as the basic gait of the Old School and of the relationship of the trot to the shoulder-in, an excellent example of a general gymnastic action. Decarpentry wrote (*L'Essentiel de la Méthode de Haute École de Raabe*, 1957, p. 94), "By imposing on a barely broken-in horse the position necessary for the effectiveness of an exercise, the Old Masters somewhat 'diverted' their horses' efforts from their natural impulsion, and this 'diversion' could not be performed without some loss of their energy. For example, for the shoulder-in, it is only in the 'holding back' of the shoulders on one side that the lateral motion of the haunches in the opposite direction can be obtained. This lateral 'jamming' necessarily absorbs a part of the output of the propulsive efforts of the hindquarters, of the forward drive.' The Old Masters, in the application their gymnastics, found themselves with the necessity 'to capture the impulsion,' following the classic expression.

To be certain, in order to conserve it sufficiently, they needed this impulsion to present a preliminary surplus, assuring a 'margin of security' such that the inevitable 'loss of speed' would have no risk of degenerating into dangerous inertia.

At the walk, the horse develops an activity insufficient to assure the impulsion, consequently the Old Masters had to resort to the use of a livelier gait: that was the trot, which, for them, was the basic gait of all their exercises."

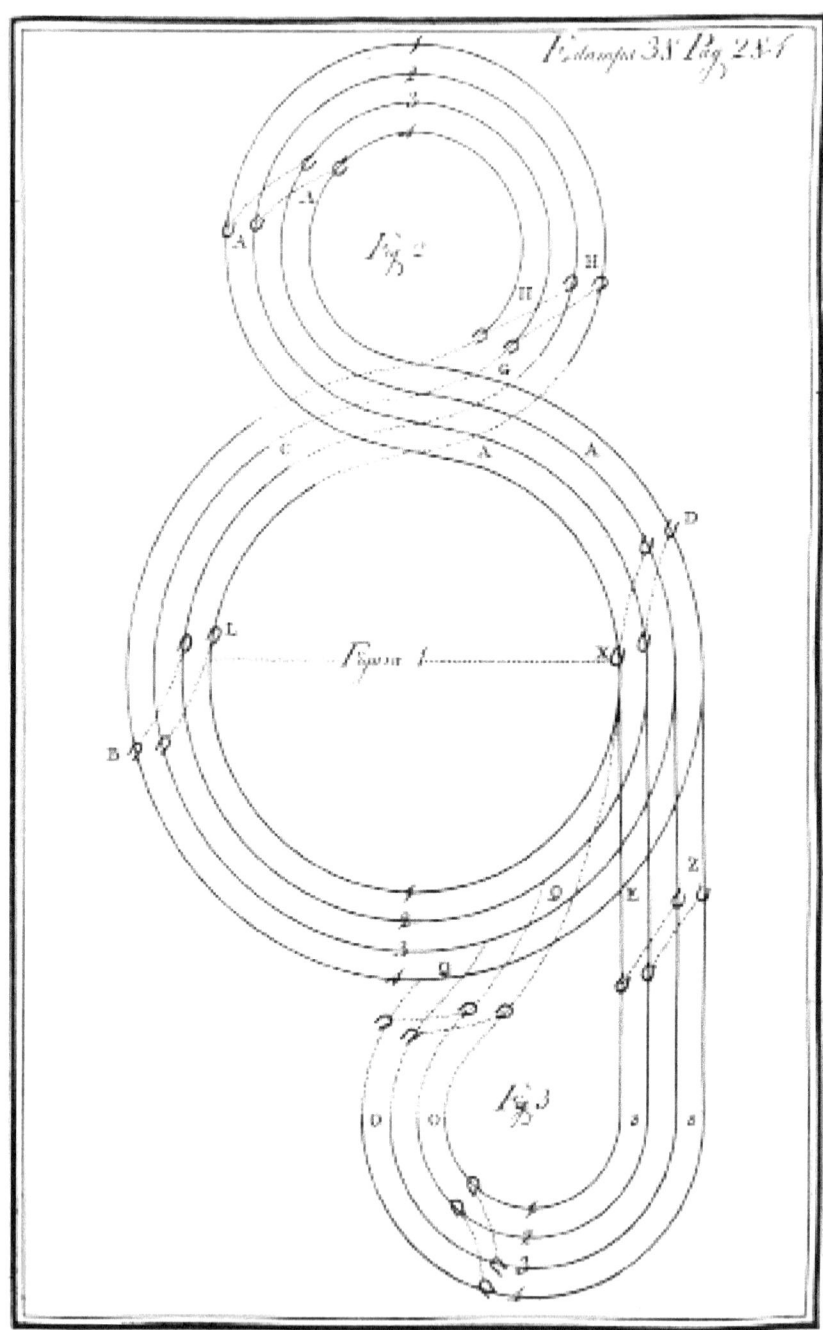

Reverse volte to the right and change of hand.

CHAPTER 2

BAUCHER'S SYSTEM

THE ANTECEDENTS

The method recommended by François Baucher did not appear in its definitive form all at once. It was constructed logically and coherently, and presented, both orally and in writing, as time went on. Baucher was unanimously considered an extraordinary teacher, one who explained to his students what he wanted them to do, or showed them himself how he wanted them to act when doubts or difficulties arose.

His written instruction was not so absolutely clear. The practical applications of certain of his details were difficult for those who could not but read the method without also hearing the advice of the master.

In 1833 he published his *Dictionnaire raisonée d'équitation* (Reasoned Dictionary of Horsemanship), in 1834 his *Dialogues sur l'Équitation* (Dialogues on Horsemanship) [See Hilda Nelson, *François Baucher, The Man and his Method*, J. A. Allen, London, 1992, P. 157], in 1837 his *Résumé complet des Principes d'Équitation servant de base à l'Éducation de toute espèce de chevaux,*(Complete Summary of the Principles of Horsemanship, Used a Base for the Education of All Sorts of Horses), in 1840 his *Passe-temps equestres* (Equestrian Diversions), in 1842 the first edition of his famous *Méthode d'Équitation basée sur de nouveaux principes*. (See Nelson, p. 95, *A Method of Horsemanship Founded upon New Principles*, 9th French edition, 2nd American edition, reprints, Hardpress, and Michigan Historical Reprint Series). This method came out in eleven successive editions comporting little change. Finally, in 1864, appeared the twelfth edition that contained some very important changes to the first system. In 1867 and 1874, there appeared the thirteenth and fourteenth editions, similar to the twelfth.

Baucher's oral teaching improved more quickly than his written instruction, since his publisher/editor, by contract, could republish the *écuyer's* work whenever he intended without asking for authorization. Identical editions succeeded the preceding ones, while Baucher was introducing many modifications into his method that he taught to his students as he went along.

Baucher's written instruction was not sufficient unto itself. Raabe declared in 1857: "The written method, the book, is not complete, sufficiently clear, lucid." (*Examen du Baucherism réduit à sa plus simple expression de M. Rul*, 1857.)

The appearance of Baucher's method was connected to his passion for dressage and for the horse. He had come to doubt the methods in use up to that time "reflecting ignorance and brutality." He said that "man has received from the Creator an intelligence superior to that of the animals, not to serve his caprices and to inflict bad treatment on them, but to receive all the services that it is right to ask of them." (*Méthode d'Équitation*, 14e éd., 1874, p. I.)

The basic reason for the modifications brought to the methods in use was the new vogue for thoroughbred horses, who served often as studs for crossbreeding.

Given the characteristic physique and spirit of most of the horses then available, the *écuyer* that applied the methods of the Old

Jardineiro, trained and ridden by DVM Guilherme Borba. Doux passage. The hand is delicate. The horse is "smiling." With a more elevated position of the neck and head, despite a temporary "diagonalization," the passage will be ameliorated.

School had, in most cases, poor success, and it is for no other reason that Comte d'Aure, in spite of being a student of Versailles, modernized his horsemanship a great deal in applying it to the outdoor horse.

To oblige the new type of horse to execute the work of the *manège*, a rational method permitting their absolute domination was necessary. The horse with round movement, a thick neck, and a large strong jaw was replaced by the long rectangular horse, made for racing, full of impulsion and strength, and the dressage of the XVIII century could not bring these animals to execute the airs of the *manège*. To François Baucher goes the honor of having conceived and developed a method that achieves this result. Baucher did not have the esteem for Iberian-bred horses that was still widespread in his era. He wrote in his *Dictionnaire* in the article entitled *RACE* (breed) (*Œuvres Complètes*, 13e éd., 1867, p. 565.), "Although my own patriotism is irritated by it, I have a preference for quality English horses; they are brilliant, proper for the *manège* and apt at every kind of exercise."

In truth, he could only adopt this position. The Old School riders continued to train horses of Iberian, Limousine, or Navarrine breed, because with their system, they could not accomplish the dressage of the new horses. It was the dressage of these new horses that Baucher undertook, inventing his method for them. The innovator, to show the advantage of his discoveries, felt the desire to contradict all that had been done before him.

BAUCHERISM AND ROMANTICISM

It is interesting to bring in parallel the appearance of Baucher's equestrian ideas with those of the concurrent ideologies of the XIX century.

In this era new ideas of romanticism arose in the arts and letters, and liberalism appeared in the economy, law, and politics. The followers of these ideas were friends and admirers of Baucher. They encouraged him to pursue his discoveries. I certainly do not mean to say that liberalism and romanticism had as doctrines, an influence on horsemanship, rather that the romantic culture and the liberal social climate with its revolutionary ideals created an innovative climate into which Baucher found himself integrated. This social atmosphere encouraged him to give form to a revolutionary form of dressage.

I did not force myself to arrive at these conclusions. In that era, *Haute École* was held in great esteem. The riders that admired it, or practiced it, were part of not only the nobility, but also of the most noted intellectual milieu. One may recall that in the dispute between Comte d'Aure and Baucher, the Duc de Nemours (a royal prince) took up the cause of the first against the partisans of the second. To the group of Baucherists, at the head of which was found the Duc d'Orléans (another royal prince brother of Nemours,) joined by many young and boisterous intellectuals. Among them the painter Delacroix, the writers Eugène Sue and Théophile Gautier, Got, of the Comédie Française (the National Theater), the musician, composer, and journalist Léon Gatayes, as well as the poet Lamartine who frequently visited the master. Baucher said to him, "See, *Haute École* is the poetry of equitation."

It was in 1842, at the most striking confrontation between Comte d'Aure's method and that of Baucher, that the latter triumphantly presented to the circus the Thoroughbred Géricault, who belonged to Lord Seymour, and was considered unmanageable. His training lasted four weeks. The evening of the presentation, Théophile Gautier, too corpulent to mount a horse, even so did not hesitate to come in person to take his place among Baucher's partisans. Foreseeing that the battle would be fierce, he exhibited the red waistcoat that he had worn twelve years beforehand at the Battle of Hernani (a Victor Hugo play that created its own controversy).

D'Aure's followers and those of Baucher engaged in a passionate polemic, as proven by the numerous brochures that it inspired. To give an idea of it, let me refer to a pamphlet by a student of Baucher, the Baron de Curnieu, entitled, "What if Baucher had never existed" With as much imagination as buffoonish verve, Curnieu holds that Baucherism is nothing other than a branch of Christianity, destroyer of ancient religions. Baucher is a mystic figure that he compares to Jesus. His loyal friends evoke the twelve apostles. After a voyage in Italy that recalls the flight from Egypt, the coming of Baucher to Paris corresponds to the entry into Jerusalem. The experience at Saumur is the temptation of Jesus by the Devil. Bringing Baucher to the highest window in the attic from where he sees the whole panorama of the "The School" – as the Devil had brought Jesus to the summit of the Mount of Olives – General de Sparre (who plays here the role of the demon, for not being a fan of the introduction of Baucherism into the army) says to Baucher, "Do not speak any more of the legs, and all this will be yours!"

If one could imagine the interest and attention that equestrian discussions aroused in the intellectuals, one might understand that Baucher, seeing the transformations realized by his friends in other domains, felt encouraged to pursue the profound reform of the old methods of dressage.

BAUCHERISM AND THE CIRCUS

In order to have an idea of the uproar around the people that we are talking about, and the events in which they were involved, one must remember that this commotion took place at the circus where performances were appreciated by elegant society. The artists who produced them were as celebrated as cinema actors or football players today. The *écuyeres* (female rider/trainers, also called *amazones*) were particularly admired and sought after. Their presentations were important acts of the show. A circus *écuyere,* Ada Menken, ignited a passion in Alexandre Dumas. Napoleon III himself and the court often came to the circus, and the Emperor went so far as to have one constructed in Paris.

Today, circus dressage is considered by certain riders to be without value, an ensemble of "tours de force" (spectacular tricks) having nothing to do with true *Haute École*. The methods used in this horsemanship that pretends to be spectacular without aspiring to perfection are most of the time artificial. But there were always some riders on *la piste* (the circus ring) presenting horses trained according to the best rules of academic dressage.

The first circus that saw the light of day in Paris, in 1767, that of Jacob Bates, was almost a *manège*, because his show was composed exclusively of equestrian performances. The circular *piste* originated there. Vaulting took advantage of it, falls to the interior of the circle being less dangerous. The diameter of 13.50 meters became standard because it was convenient to all the artists and their horses to keep the same dimension for all the circuses.

Even if during these early times of the circus, the shows were almost entirely composed of equestrian acts, one could not say that they drew their merit from true dressage.

True dressage began to appear in the circus at the beginning of the XIX century when Antonio Franconi (1737 – 1836), a trainer of big cats, set himself to train horses. His son, Laurent Franconi (1776 – 1849), in turn trained and presented horses. As General L'Hotte said, he was "majesty on a horse." He could, as far as his presentations were concerned, serve as a model for Baucher, who never attained Franconi's presence.

It was in the golden age of the circus that Baucher made his appearance. In France and abroad, he presented horses trained in his method, and this is how he became known.

Would the person who scorns circus dressage on principle ponder the quality of dressage necessary to make the horse enter a ring where, disquieted by the public that surrounds him, blinded by the lights, deafened by the noise, he must execute exercises that we all know to be already very difficult "in the silence of the *manège?*"

If one would be willing to remember the airs that Baucher invented and showed in the circus ring, one could ask the reason for the scorn expressed in the past, or today, with respect to the circus *écuyers*. And should one invite contemporary riders to present these airs, in their turn, on the same *piste*[38], perhaps one might receive an evasive response. We must resign ourselves to only imagine the demonstration they would make!

It is regrettable that higher dressage is not shown today in the circus. It loses thereby the sole possibility that higher dressage has to be shown as often and freely as possible, as it was with the Franconis, the Bauchers, the Fillises, who acquired their celebrity at the circus.

It is interesting to note that in our day, the best Portuguese riders do not look down on presenting their school horses at the circus. José Martins Queiroz de Monténégro (Minotes) went to Paris to appear at an evening performance for the fans of the Cirque Molier. The José Manuel da Cunha Menezes – father and son – João Gallardi Conde de Fontalva (whose personal *manége*, in the form of a circle, was as large as the Coliseum), Joaquim Gonçalves de Miranda, Roberto de Vasconcellos, and lastly, Nuno Oliveira have presented at the circus some high school horses trained by them according to traditional equestrian principles.

Frederico da Cunha was the first Portuguese rider to receive lessons from Baucher himself, in Paris. He came back to Portugal in 1844. He was *Écuyer* to the Royal Household.

---

38 Track, the outside track of the circus ring, circus ring.

Baucher at the circus on Capitaine

I have heard it said that Antonio de Figueiredo was also a student of Baucher, but Salvador José da Costa, in his *Susbidios para a Historia da Equitação* (Contribution to the History of Equitation), wrote that Antonio de Figueiredo was a disciple of Frederico da Cunha, himself a student of the French Master. However, since Antonio da Figueiredo worked in France from 1853 to 1856, with the best *écuyers*; it is possible that he had been initiated into Baucherism by its inventor himself.

BAUCHER'S TEACHING METHODS, FIRST MANNER

The concept of School horsemanship as it has been set out by Baucher is essentially different from that of the horsemanship of the XVIII century. Eighteenth Century horsemanship had the goals of training the exercises of the low school first, then airs above the ground and school jumps. Baucher intended to perfect the natural gaits, and those that derive from them.

What is the principle that serves as the base of his method? This one: to substitute the instinctive forces of the horse with the forces transmitted to the horse by the rider. This rule expressed in this way was naturally the butt of the most acerbic critics, because one cannot say that the rider transmits any forces to the horse. Instead, he puts the forces of the horse into action and directs them. Baucher modified this excessive wording of his principle. And we find under his pen the expression of forces "combated," "moderated," "used," "directed," and "harmonized."

What is the true significance of the principle? Let us cite General Decarpentry: "To suppress any initiative by the horse in the use of his forces, the rider alone determining and regulating that use, only in the measure and form established by him, without according the least expression to the instinct of the horse, not in the production, nor in the mode of his activity." (*Baucher et son École*, 1948, p. 44. [*Baucher and His School*, Xenophon Press 2011])

"The fundamental principle of Baucher aimed, in its practical application, by means of the '*effet d'ensemble*,' to completely dominate the horse, without shutting him down. It was with horses Baucherised in this way that the Master gave the dazzling exhibitions that made him a celebrity, over the course of which he presented about thirty new airs that gave the horse's work a variety and sparkle totally unknown before then." (Decarpentry, *Baucher...* 1948, p. 62.)

The Techniques

Baucher's low school had the goal of preparing the horse in the gaits or in the airs of *Haute École*, in a different way from what took place in the Old School.

His fundamental technique was the *effet d'ensemble* that allowed the rider to annul the instinctive forces.

How did Baucher discover "the fixed hand" necessary to the application of this technique? Here is what he said (*Œuvres Complètes*, 13ᵉ éd., 1867, p. 623.): "I was in Le Havre and I was going home, one day from the horse fair with a horse for which I had paid 300 francs. My quick examination had embraced the whole ensemble of the horse, and, upon return to the *manège*, I attentively examined my horse's mouth, and recognized with sadness that the thickness of the gums on his bars explained the enormous resistance that he offered to the action of the bit. Time after time, I applied the most powerful brakes, and the mouth remained insensitive. Could it be something else about his conformation?"

"One day, as I recall, I rode *Bienfaisant* (Good willing) as the gentleness of his character had made me name him, and I stopped myself in the *manège*. I was reflecting, and while my mind was working, my hand remained fixed. All at once, I felt *Bienfaisant* light. *Bienfaisant* had yielded. *Bienfaisant* was not resisting anymore! So what had happened? Since there is no effect without a cause, I recognized that the fixity of my hand had brought about the yielding of the horse, and I got proof that the mouth was for nothing in the resistances, and that they came from contractions in the neck, because I had obviously not modified the anatomy of the bars, I had not reduced their thickness."

"Such was the debut of the method. *Bienfaisant* had taught me that there are no hard mouths, no insensitive bars."

***Effet d'ensemble* and *rassembler*.** What is the *effet d'ensemble* ("coordinated effect")? It consists of the simultaneous use of the impulsive aids and the holding aids, in a fashion that the opposition of forces obtained by those aids leads to the complete annulment of these forces.

To get to the *effet d'ensemble* on the horse, whether in place, or in movement, one gymnasticizes the forehand and the hindquarters by what are called the "flexions." The direct flexion is prepared for by the lateral flexions that provoke the relaxation (*decontraction*) of the jaw and the *ramener*. To the lateral flexions acting on the forehand, correspond the mobilizations of the croup that facilitate the engagement of the hind legs.

The horse is even prepared for the rein-back by these exercises. That is because Baucher was not content to make the hand an uncrossable barrier; he also gave it the power to provoke the horse to walk to the rear.

**Cantador, trained and ridden by René Bacharach.
Lesson in the piaffe. The beautiful *tride* of a Portuguese horse.**

It is appropriate to carefully differentiate *"effet d'ensemble"* from *"rassembler,"* which is not so easy from only reading Baucher's works. Much confusion has arisen and many errors have been committed by those who only read the illustrious master, without also attending his lessons.

In the *rassembler*, the rider's legs act with alternating little pushes; in the *effet d'ensemble*, they act with simultaneous and prolonged pressure.

In the *rassembler*, the hands have an intermittent action that delicately restrains the forehand, while in the *effet d'ensemble*, the hand has a continuous holding action.

Raabe compared the sensation that he experienced on a horse that he submitted to the *effet d'ensemble* with that felt by a man who holds the hand of a boisterous child. The man subordinates the pressure of his hand to the movements of the hand that he has in his own, this for the purpose of dominating it. There comes a moment where the held hand merely conforms to the indications of the hand that holds it.

Baucher's preoccupation in the *effet d'ensemble* and in the *rassembler* was the mode of action of the rider's legs, while Raabe preoccupied himself with the location of their action – whether at the girth, for the *effet d'ensemble*, or behind the girth on the flanks, for the *rassembler* and for impulsion.

In his First Manner, Baucher assured the canter departs with the leg opposite to the lead and the rein on the side of the requested lead. In the same way, he used the leg opposite to and the rein on the inside for voltes and changes of hand.

The goal of the *rassembler* is to obtain great mobility in all directions, thanks to the reduction in the horse's base of support. The *rassembler* is only sought after the horse is in complete *ramener*.

The *ramener* practiced by Baucher during the first phase of his equestrian thinking put the horse's head in a vertical position. It has been sometimes criticized for exceeding even this position in the *rassembler* "in place" that he used at that time. The narrowing of the horse's base came from the considerable bringing together of the fore and hind legs that he demanded. The fact that the horse was under himself in front caused this position of the head behind the vertical, and one can understand that many of the "followers" of Baucherism would not be able to avoid it.

This position of *rassembler*, which the detractors compared to that of a cat that humps his back, had the purpose of creating an equal distribution of weight on the shoulders and on the haunches. The consequence was a style of piaffe and passage in which the fore and hind legs rose to the same height.

Baucher, during the greatest part of his career, used working in hand only for the preparation of the flexions of the jaw and neck. It was only after the accident that broke both his legs that he pushed work in hand further, extending it to pirouettes, and to the *rassembler* all the way to piaffe while using the longe whip. (Decarpentry, *Équitation*

Academic, 1949, p. 280.) [*Academic Equitation*, J. A. Allen, London, 1971, Trafalgar Square Publishing, North Pomfret, 2001] The *rassembler* of which we are speaking, that of the First Manner, was obtained with the horse ridden.

As to *ramener* of the Second Manner, it was obtained first in hand, by flexions of the neck consecutive to the relaxation of the jaw after maximum elevation of the neck and head, even getting to a nearly horizontal position of the head.

Decarpentry (*L'Essentiel de la Méthode de Haute École de Raabe*, 1957, pp. 148 – 149.) envisioned the elevation of the neck and head, by intermittent action of the hand, only if the horse presents resistances of weight, ducks down behind the bit, over bends, or puts himself on the shoulders. The half-halts are performed by means of an isolated rein on the convex side of the neck (outside rein).

The walk is the basic gait. And that is understandable, because a horse does not submit to the *effet d'ensemble* perfectly except in place or in a slow walk.

As soon as lightness is lost, the rider must halt the horse and relax him (by asking for the yielding of the jaw) so as to depart again with a light horse. In the beginning, the sole means of obtaining lightness is to alternate halt and walk. Since the movement of the horse "being much less, he is ready to feel more easily the various impressions that one communicates to him in order to position him correctly, and on this favorable position (in which he is light) depends the grace and precision of all of his movements." (Baucher, *Œuvres Complètes*, 13e éd., 1867, p. 548.)

According to the Baucher method, the more legs there are on the ground at the same time, the easier it will be to balance the horse. It is therefore at the halt or the walk that the horse must be gymnasticized. The Old School riders, on the other hand, had adopted the trot as the basic gait.

I think the rider who does not possess the tact of a Baucher must alternate the trot with the walk, because the movement in the trot is more energetic and the resistances are felt better. That does not mean that the perfection of work at the walk does not remain the base of all training, nor that there have not been *écuyers* who could train their mounts with only this gymnastic, such as Lubersac, of whom they said that he worked at the walk for eighteen months to two years, and that, at the end of that period, his horses were "finished" at all gaits.

According to La Guérinière, the work at the trot was also essential to set the neck. It deters the neck's tendency to be too flexible, a tendency frequently encountered in the horses of the Old School, as we can see in their descendants, our peninsular horses. The Old School therefore, was, in fact, correct to adopt the trot as the basic gait.

Another innovation by Baucher was to consider **lightness as the essential quality** of all School work, and his research brought him to the conclusion that lightness was as much the cause as the effect of general equilibrium of the horse. One must not lose sight that the rigorous concept of lightness includes not only the mobilization of the lower jaw, provoked by the movements made by the tongue, as in swallowing, but also the facility with which the horse obeys the least indication of the legs.

To obtain total lightness, Baucher separately gymnasticized the jaw, the neck, the poll, the shoulders, the spinal column, the legs, etc., thus practicing what he called *partial actions*, separating himself again on this point from the Old School who proceeded by *general actions*.

One could say that Baucher used the tactic of a military leader who orders isolated actions against the enemy towards the end of obtaining the final victory more easily.

The *partial actions*, a fundamental point in Baucherist dressage, consists of relaxing (decontracting) a chosen part of the body without letting other parts of the body participate in the executed movement. For example, the rider flexes the jaw in such a way that the horse remains immobile. He gymnasticizes the croup or the shoulders by displacing them, step by step from one side to the other, so that the head and neck remain as immobile as possible. When they are practiced in these ways, a *partial action* (exercise) produces the correct result.

The *partial actions* are: the flexions of the jaw, poll, and neck; the reverse pirouettes (around the shoulders); the pirouettes (around the hindquarters).

One consequence of this method is that in the lateral movements, the crossing of the hind legs is very pronounced.

The piaffe is started quite early as a normal consequence of the practice of the *rassembler*.

Therefore, the piaffe does not come from the School trot being collected to the point of being executed without advancing, instead, it is the direct result of the successive posing of the diagonals in place.

Captain Raabe separated himself from Baucher on the manner of obtaining the piaffe. In effect, he got there by reducing the length of the trot stride, preserving the rhythm, until its execution in place. (Decarpentry, *L'Essentiel de la Méthode de Haute École de Raabe*, 1957, p. 119.)

With both of these techniques, the horse in piaffe, raises his fore and hind legs to the same height. "It is surprising that Baucher persisted in this prescription of equal height for the legs, after having, in his last manner, prescribed the elevation of the forehand, as well as a disposition of the ensemble of the horse's body that very much approached the position given by the Old Masters to their horses." (Decarpentry, *Équitation Academique*, 1949, p. 202.)

In the effet d'ensemble, the legs or the spurs, acting simultaneously, are used together with the hand, which acts upward. In the *rassembler*, the legs or the spurs, acting alternately, are used conjointly with the hand, which softly holds the front. (Faverot de Kerbrech, *Dressage Méthodique du Cheval de Selle...*, 1891, pp. 11, 98, 169.) [*Methodical Dressage of the Riding Horse*, Xenophon Press, 2010]

In the First Manner the spurs were fitted with rowels with sharp points.

BAUCHER'S TEACHING METHODS, SECOND MANNER

General L'Hotte wrote (*Un Officier de Cavalerie*, 1905, p. 105), "Baucher's discoveries always brought out, in him, this particular attitude: the latest line of thought eclipsed all that had preceded it, and represented, in his eyes, the last word in equitation." One finds confirmation of this idea in Baucher's own words to his student L'Hotte that the latter reported (*Loc. cit.,* p. 125): "If, at this moment, you would ride my old horses, Partisan, Capitaine, Neptune, Buridan, so admired at the time, you would find them not to be trained, so great is the difference that separates them from my horses of today."

Diogo de Bragança on Rio.
The piaffe is one of the most beautiful expressions of the *rassembler*.

Before analyzing the modifications brought by Baucher to his First Manner, it is appropriate to examine the reasons that drove him there.

One of them, independent of his own will, was the accident that crushed him cruelly, in 1855, while he was working a horse in the ring at the circus. The chandelier at the top of the big tent suddenly fell on him. He had his right leg broken, the left hip and knee dislocated, with grave contusions to the chest, shoulders and lower back.

In other respects, Baucher never ceased to be preoccupied by the errors committed by his students when applying what was called the "New Method," principally in the *effet d'ensemble* by the hand and spurs. The subjection to which the horse was submitted had the great inconvenience of deadening him to the spur, of extinguishing his impulsion, when the master himself was not riding the horse, or when his principles were not being applied exactly.

Therefore as a result of the disaster that had diminished his physical capabilities, and because he saw that his students often found it impossible to apply the "method" without making grave errors, Baucher brought modifications to the procedures that he had first adopted. His principles, meanwhile, remained the same; the final goal of his dressage remained identical to that of the First Manner. Only the methods of application would change – sometimes, it must be said, quite profoundly.

VioláceoI, trained by Nuno Oliveira, ridden by René Bacharach. Passage. Descent of the hand. The horse goes as if by himself.

The Techniques

The base of the method still rested on the *effet d'ensemble* and the *mise en main*. To obtain the *mise en main*, to realize the relaxation of the jaw that brought the face to the vertical, Baucher in the beginning had lightened the forehand, shifting part of its weight toward the hindquarters by rolling the neck, even putting the head inside the vertical. Now, in the new manner, the *mise en main* is still obtained by lifting the forehand and shifting part of its weight toward the hindquarters. But this time, Baucher began by raising the neck and relaxing the jaw with the face above the vertical, sometimes even brought up to horizontal.

The *ramener* continues to be required but, to close the head-neck angle, Baucher, instead of bringing the head to the body as he did in the First Manner, pushed the body towards the head, which is placed as high as possible. The lowering of the face to the vertical then results from the progressive engagement of the haunches.

In summary, things were as follows:

In the First Manner, one began with the *ramener*. In the Second Manner**, the ramener is the consequence of the elevation** of the front end and the advance of the body of the horse to meet the forehand. The *ramener* ceases to be, as it was at the beginning, a position of the head independent of the general position of the body (First Manner), to become a consequence of the balance of the horse.

The effet d'ensemble is sought now with great precaution by delicate actions of the hand and legs. It ceases to be the habitual means to re-establish lost lightness. It becomes, in fact, the infallible procedure for domination, and is used only rarely.

Lightness is obtained by the hand alone: vibrations to destroy resistances of force (muscular tension in the jaw and neck), half-halts to annul the resistances of weight (balance), by shifting the weight from the forehand to the hindquarters.

The rule is established assigning **the legs to give impulsion**, and the hand to give direction and lightness, from where the new Baucherist principle: "hand without legs, legs without hand."

If Baucher had come to recommend the alternating use of the aids, it was because of the perpetual contradiction in the legs and hand of the rider "who is always disposed to attribute to the horse those faults that the simultaneous use of his legs and hand make him commit." (*Œuvres Complètes, 13ᵉ éd.*, 1867, p. 174.) And Baucher even defined the *effet d'ensemble*, which by then he used only as an exception, to be followed by a depart to the trot on an action of the legs, and even the spurs, without any opposition by the hand.

The voltes and turns are now demanded on the rein of opposition (neck rein), with the inside rein acting to maintain lightness. To set the haunches, Baucher added to these aids the use of the inside leg, and even the outside rein.

For the canter departs, he preferred the leg on the side of the requested lead. In the voltes and the work on two tracks, he also made the inside leg predominate.

In the change of lead at the canter, Baucher finished by using the leg and rein on the inside, whereas in the First Manner, he used the outside leg.

The flexions and the work with the whip diminished in importance in that part of the training concerning the relaxation of the jaw and the neck, an aspect of the First Manner that had often been pushed to an exaggeration.

Another important innovation consisted of **the decomposition of the force and the movement**.

If the horse resists in movement, the rider halts him, calms him, obtains relaxation (of the jaw), and it is only after this, that he restarts the exercise that was in the course of execution. Every time that there is a loss of balance that the horse manifests by his resistances (he tightens up, he becomes crooked, etc.), the rider must proceed in a similar way. This innovation is so efficient as to bring into lightness any mute, stiff, or poorly balanced horses that Faverot de Kerbrech counseled decomposing the force and the movement as often as it is necessary. (*Dressage Méthodique du Cheval de Selle*...,1891, p. 57. [*Methodical Dressage of the Riding Horse AND Dressage of the Outdoor Horse*, Xenophon Press 2010])

One preoccupation of each moment in dressage must be to practice **descents[39] of the hand, descents of the legs, and simultaneous**

---

39 Yielding

The word "passage" comes from the Italian word "*passegio.*"
[to promenade]

descents of the hand and legs.

In the *descent of the hand*, the rider progressively abandons the reins on the neck with his mount conserving the acquired position by himself. The gait continues with the same cadence and the same lightness. It must be the same in the *descent of the legs* when they abandon contact with the flanks.

A horse's dressage reaches its apogee, according to Baucher and Faverot de Kerbrech, when in the simultaneous *descent of the hand and legs*, the horse conserves the cadence, lightness, collection, and brilliance into which he was brought with the help of the aids.

Baucher did not use spurs with sharpened rowels anymore; the points had been removed. He even came to ride without spurs. This was what he called "equitation in slippers."

As to the bit that Baucher had used at the beginning, he modified it, having found it to be too severe, by reducing the length of the shanks and replacing the curb chain by a strap simply taking its point of support under the chin groove.

Later, he did not use anything but a simple bridoon. Several days before his death, he still recommended its use, according to Colonel L'Hotte (who was promoted to General a year after the death of his venerated master, "…You will see," Baucher said to him, "that it is *plein de belles choses* (full of good things, of completely beneficial use)." (L'Hotte, *Un Officier de Cavalerie*, 1905, p. 255.)

EXAMINATION OF BAUCHER'S METHODS

After having analyzed Baucher's techniques and their evolution, it is appropriate to examine his method and to evaluate it.

Many criticisms have been made by notable riders. Without wanting now to discuss the value of the criticisms by Seeger, Steinbrecht, d'Aure, Fillis, Salins, etc., I will nevertheless bring up the words of Gerhardt, student of the first method, on the subject of the German Old School.

Gerhardt wrote (*La Vérité sur la Méthode Baucher ancienne et nouvelle*, 1869) that the German Christoff Jacob Liebens published a *Reitbuch*, in Leipzig, in 1665, that contained the same principles as Baucherism, and that another German, Louis Hünersdorf, Master Rider to HRH the Prince of Hesse, published in Cassel, in 1791, a work in which is found the techniques that allow one to think that Hünersdorf was also a precursor to Baucher. (The 6th edition of this work was translated into French by the Belgian Captain A. de Brochowsky and published in Brussels, in 1843, under the title *Équitation Allemande. Méthode la plus facile et la plus naturelle pour dresser le Cheval d'Officier et d'Amateur* [German Horsemanship. The Easiest and most Natural Method of training the Horse for the Officer and the Amateur.]) The fact that these two German works appeared, one of them a hundred and seventy nine years and the other fifty three years, before the "New

Baucher, *Souvenirs Équestres.* **Capitaine at the piaffe.**

Method," (first published in 1844), contain the concepts and techniques claimed by Baucher does not allow us to accuse the latter of plagiarism. In fact, Gerhardt wrote (*La Vérité sur la Méthode Baucher ancienne et nouvelle*, 1869, p. 102.), that despite appearances "...nothing proves that M. Baucher had copied anything: he had simply discovered a collection of truths that, without his knowledge, were contained in the German Old School, and he has considerably perfected its practical application."

Let us then examine this collection of truths, trying to avoid those obscurities so numerous in Baucher's own writings, to explore the clearer explanations provided by his more celebrated disciples.

WALK, THE GAIT AT THE BASE OF DRESSAGE

The walk is the basic gait of dressage because precision in the execution of the rider's commands is required from the beginning of the progression, and because the horse can then evaluate these commands only if they are given at sufficiently spaced intervals. Their sequencing should not provoke any brusque reaction in the horse that is receiving them.

The work at the walk is itself prepared for by a series of exercises asked for in place.

The advantages of work at the walk were laid out by General Decarpentry (*L'Essentiel de la Méthode de Haute École de Raabe*, 1957, p. 95.): "Absolute mastery of the play of all four legs avoids nearly all of the difficulties that are, for example, presented by the engagement of the hind legs in the *rassembler*.

"The assured conservation of their uninterrupted mobility forward, to the rear, and in place leads directly to cadence."

"A horse familiarized with departs at the walk started on a specified foreleg will depart correctly at the canter on the same signal, accompanied by an appropriate impulsive action (of the leg)."

"Experienced at the exercise of 'changing the step,' he executes as a 'natural' result the change of lead at the canter, for which he has been prepared, on the other hand, by changes of direction on both one and two tracks started on the foreleg on the side of the new direction."

THE POSITION OF THE HORSE'S HEAD

AT THE BEGINNING OF DRESSAGE

In the First Manner, it is the verticality of the forehead that is sought after before all else, and it is with the head so placed that the other parts of the body are gymnasticized. In the Second Manner, the head is placed as high as possible; the forehead can even be lifted to the horizontal, the relaxation of the jaw being obtained more rapidly in this position. It is only after that phase that the horse gathers himself with his neck in the suitably elevated position.

The good position that the horse must take up for the purpose of dressage is still the same. The haunches lower, the hind legs engage, the loins are flexible, the jaw is relaxed, the neck comes up and bends at the poll, the forehead approaches the vertical, etc. It is the silhouette of a trained horse. The means employed to obtain this silhouette are multiple. They differ according to the school, according to the tact of each rider. Above all, they are a function of the conformation and temperament of each horse.

Yet, as it concerns Baucherism, even if one or the other manner allows the rider to achieve a good dressage, I believe that in certain cases, it is necessary to have recourse to the First Manner.

To systematically elevate the head of a horse with a thick neck, especially if he has mediocre and weak hindquarters, is to provoke, it seems to me, the lowering of the withers, and the shifting of the weight of the body toward the croup, excessively burdens the hindquarters which are generally less developed than the forehand.

This situation is commonly presented with horses from the Iberian Peninsula. They often have a substantial forehand (strong neck, large head, and prominent jaw) with proportionately less developed hindquarters. We must not excessively burden this part of the horse by elevating the head and neck. If we did that, we would squash the haunches and take away all their mobility. What is more, with such animals, even with the head very high and the relaxation of the jaw, it does not necessarily follow that the *ramener* would be obtained.

By what techniques then, are we to position the horse? By the flexions of the neck and the jaw starting from a position in which the forehead is vertical. This position is favorable to the engagement of the hindquarters. The rider should try to make the hind legs advance progressively under the body. Only after that should he try to raise the forehand up to the position that his conformation allows the horse to support. This way we avoid the surcharge of the hindquarters by the weight of the heavier parts of the horse's body, which are the neck and the head, and thus we arrive at placing the latter in a correct position that facilitates the engagement of the hindquarters.

Concerning Iberian Peninsula horses, that have an innate propensity to the *rassembler*, one must work them while keeping their forehand in a position close to that which is one of the components of the *rassembler*. The rider will ameliorate this position still more by alternating shortened movements, which are easier for these horses, with more ample movements.

It will generally be necessary to proceed in the opposite way with Thoroughbreds.

Le Florido, trained and ridden by M. de Nestier, *écuyer* to Louis XV, model of academic equitation. The engraving illustrates the moment of halt from the very collected canter to the right, the horse obeying a (light) indication. One may note the very short shanks of the curb bit, said to be "à la Nestier."

Iran, trained and ridden by Captain Sainte Phalle. The horse in canter to the right, is in the same excellent position. Although ridden in a simple snaffle, it would be preferable that there be less rein tension.

The techniques that we have described are those of Baucher's First Manner. It is recommended that one watch the relative positions of the forehand and the hindquarters so that impulsion is not perturbed. This is very important because there is no doubt that the principal stumbling block of Baucherism is the excessive use of the techniques which were invented, and used with tact, by Baucher himself.

In truth, the "New Method" was a double-edged sword. It permitted absolute subjugation of the horse. However, the position by which one obtained it was not without problems, because it could provoke *acculement* (backing up, sucking back, and coming behind the bit) or at least "extinguish" an animal that had fire and natural impulsion.

These setbacks have often been the fate of those who have wanted to practice Baucherism without having carefully measured the scope of its techniques. Baucher's well-loved disciple, Louis Rul expressed it in this way: "It would take a book to write about all the burlesque, ridiculous, *à contre-poil* (against the grain) applications that I have seen of the method. One rider has so confounded the functions of legs and hands that the horse backs up instead of going forward... and yet he has applied the Baucher method! Another has so lowered the neck that his horse resembles a truffle hunter more than man's beautiful conquest! 'Baucher's Method!' Another fan, fresh out of college, who believes himself a rider because he has twice used his twenty-four lesson tickets for the *manège*, also wants to practice the Baucher Method. Oh! Surprise! His horse neither advances nor backs up, but turns in place with the rapidity of a Hindustani pearl threader. 'Satanic Method!' A fourth has so unequally distributed the weight that his horse, instead of going straight, incessantly travels in a diagonal line. One would believe seeing one of these collegians ambulating, with blindfolded eyes, on the lawn at Versailles. '*E semper* the Baucher method!'" (*Le Baucherism réduit à sa plus simple expression*, 1857, pp 2 and 3. "Baucherism reduced to its simplest expression".)

In the Second Manner, laid out in an ideal fashion in General Faverot de Kerbrech's book (*Dressage Méthodique du Cheval de Selle, d'après les derniers enseignements de F. Baucher, recueillis par un de ses élèves*, 1891 [*Methodical Dressage of the Riding Horse,* Xenophon Press 2010]), the maximum elevation of the neck is prescribed. An illustration of the dressage effected by following this progression is given to us by the impressive and even stupefying photographs of Beudant.

We have already brought to light some of the objections to the Second Manner, in the preceding pages and earlier when we spoke of the limits of the *ramener*. We are going to add some considerations taken from texts written by the best students of Baucher's Second Manner.

First of all General L'Hotte, who had practiced both the First and Second Manner, said to us (*Questions Équestres*, 1906, p. 177. [Equestrian Questions]), "The experienced *écuyer* moreover knows that he must not seek the *rassembler* until he has the *ramener.* If he engages the hocks under the body prematurely, his hands would no longer feel the opposition in the direction of the impulsion that is necessary for them to be able to vanquish the resistances characteristic of the front end."

General Faverot practiced the *ramener outré* [excessive ramener, behind the vertical] in place, at all three gaits, etc., and Captain Beudant advised (*Mains sans Jambes...,* 1945, p.45. "Hands without Legs"), "Go from the three gaits to the rein-back, and forward again, often, while remaining in *ramener outré*."

A rider, having acquired some practice in this technique, is brought to the following consideration: if at the end of lessons (with the neck and head being elevated to the maximum, by means of half-halts or some other manner, even up to a horizontal face, with the horse being worked in hand or mounted, at the halt or in movement,) frequent transitions from one gait to another are made in *ramener outré*, even if they only last a quarter or a fifth of the lesson, they will have more effectiveness than any other technique because the *ramener outré* is a means of unquestionable domination.

It was not only by the systematic maximum elevation of the head and by obtaining a certain mobility of the jaw that Beudant achieved the really fantastic results revealed by his photographs. When I see that some followers of the dressage described by Faverot do not use *ramener outré*, I conclude that they are not practicing this dressage in its totality. What is worse, they neglect one of its more effective exercises.[40]

In effect, Faverot said to us, "The *elevation of the neck* combined with the *ramener outré* gives and fixes the correct position of the head, which from then on, it never loses neither in the extended gaits nor in difficult movements." (*Dressage Méthodique du Cheval de Selle...*, 1891, p. 187.) [*Methodical Dressage of the Riding Horse*, Xenophon Press 2010]

Those who recognize the effectiveness of these two actions (*elevation of the neck* and *ramener outré*) know that it is the latter that allows the obtained position never to be lost.

But one must not forget when one embarks upon the *ramener outré*, this important recommendation from Faverot: "This work must never be undertaken unless the rider can easily obtain the maximum and sustained elevation of the neck at the walk, trot, and canter, with lightness, the jaw yielding from the beginning without movement of the head."

FLEXIONS

Early Baucherism is accused of flexing the jaw with the face behind the vertical. Even if the illustrations of the early editions of Baucher's work confirm this assertion, the text of the sixth edition (1844) of the *Méthode d'Équitation* says (p. 158), "...make the horse understand that the perpendicular position of his head is the only one that remains permitted to him under the hand of the rider," a statement which is in fact quite different.

---

40 There were evidently exceptions. It is certain that with a horse like the mare *Hamïa* whose neck was too short and thick for the ramener to be possible, Beudant, *a fortiori*, did not practice the *ramener outré*. That did not prevent him from achieving an extremely complete and brilliant dressage from *Hamïa*. There is good reason to suppose, to cite another example, that one of the Chief Riders of the Vienna School, Max von Weyrother, had perfectly submissive horses. The beautiful equestrian portrait of him that we know (A, Podhajsky, *Die Spanische Hofreitschule*, 1948, p. XXV) shows him at the school canter on a horse with a massive neck, not in ramener. (N.F.T.)

We read in the *Manuel d'Équitation* ("Manual of Horsemanship") by Gerhardt in 1859 (p. 97, note I.) "We insist essentially on the vertical position of the head and on an elevated neck. We consider as defective any position of the head deviating from this line, especially behind the vertical." We find the same idea in Raabe (Decarpentry, *L'Essentiel de la Méthode de Haute École de Raabe*, 1957.); we read (p. 81.) *à propos* of the beginning of *rassembler*: "The rider... leaves the horse free to take the elevation of the head that is convenient to him," and (p. 65.) *à propos* of a horse that forces the hand: "When that happens, the rider fixes the hand without pulling. That way he erects a barrier that must prevent the horse from going above the vertical, but not to come behind the vertical."

Finally on the subject of lateral flexions – which Baucher, at the beginning, exaggerated without a doubt – Raabe recommended progressive lateral placement so that an excessive incurvation would not have any effect on the croup. For the action to be *partial*, it must be limited to a lateral flexion at the poll.

RASSEMBLER AT THE HALT IN THE FIRST MANNER

This effect consists of combining a pronounced *ramener* with an advance of the hind legs under the body until they almost touch the front feet. This position "of a mountain goat on a peak" is less artificial than it appears, because a horse eating grass in a field or his hay in the stable sometimes takes it up himself. Besides, it is an excellent gymnastic of the back and the loins. Doesn't the use of the "Chambon" make the horse take on this position in movement?

The *rassembler* at the halt according to the First Manner is an exercise, and does not constitute the position of a trained horse. This exercise must not leave a trace in the finished horse. That was a difficulty encountered by those who had read Baucher without having received his lessons directly.

The portrayals of Baucher, made during his life, of the piaffe of Partisan and Buridan, as well as at the lengthened trot and the "parade" on Capitaine leave one only to suppose that for each, the *attitude* [position], most correct, has benefited from the gymnastic of the *rassembler* at the halt.

"HAND WITHOUT LEGS, LEGS WITHOUT HAND"

Baucher defined the *rassembler* at the halt from the First Manner – that he called "*effet d'ensemble*" ("coordinated effect") and that must not be confused with the *effet d'ensemble* from the Second Manner – as a "continuous force that is equally opposed between the hand and the legs." It "must precede and follow each exercise in the graduated limit that is assigned to it." (*Méthode d'Équitation*, 6ᵉ éd., 1844, p. 160.)

In the second phase of Baucherism that Faverot described, he said (*Dressage Méthodique de Cheval de Selle...*, 1891, p. 31. [*Methodical Dressage of the Riding Horse*, Xenophon Press 2010]), "The goal of the *effet d'ensemble* is to immobilize the horse or to force him to keep the gait and direction desired." In the first phase, the *effet d'ensemble* is sought directly, as soon as the horse is sufficiently flexed, while in the second, it does not intervene until after the flexions followed by the application of the principle "hand without legs, legs without hand."

The appearance of the principle "hand without legs, legs without hand" in the twelfth edition (1864) of *Méthode d'Équitation*[41] provoked this exclamation from Gerhardt: "Then Baucher is no longer Baucher!" But his alarm appeared to be excessive, because, as L'Hotte specified, the formula in the beginning was applied only to everyday horsemanship to obviate the bad results obtained by insufficiently experienced riders who applied the *effet d'ensemble* outside of the presence of the master.

In more advanced dressage, the use of the principle "hand without legs, legs without hand" is somewhat theoretical, so that if one refers to its interpretation by General Decarpentry, it resembles an *effet d'ensemble* sought after with great precaution: "If the hand acts or increases the intensity of its action, the leg should either maintain the same intensity of its action or decrease it, as the case requires. However, the leg should never increase its action while the hand is acting or increasing its action". (*Piaffer et Passage*, 1932, p. 11) [*Piaffer and Passage*, 1961, Van Nostrand edition, pp. 10-11.]

In fact, if the *effet d'ensemble*, according to Faverot, has the role of requiring the horse to "conserve the gait and direction desired," it

---

41 In his *Méthode de Haute École d'Équitation*, 1863, Raabe, student of Baucher, had already spoken (p. 160), in (the section on) the reverse pirouette, about the mobilization of the haunches by the rider's legs, without the intervention of the hand. (N.F.T.)

retains then, in the Second Manner, its principal role.

The principle "hand without legs, legs without hand" once again evolved with Beudant. One of his books, published in 1945 is entitled, "*Main sans Jambes...*" ("Hand without Legs..."). Why was this principle, revealed by Baucher, reduced in this way? Why did Beudant prefer to leave the second part unstated? René Bacharach posed that very question to this *écuyer* without equal who had achieved such finesse in the aids. Beudant responded, "Because, if the hand is well used, one has, so to say, no need for the legs."

Beudant had already explained this opinion in the first edition (1929) of his *Dressage du Cheval de Selle*. He cites there, under the heading "*La main fixe*" (The fixed hand) (p. 59), the ultimate recommendation that Baucher, on his deathbed, made to his student Colonel L'Hotte (the recommendation was reported by General L'Hotte in *Un Officier de Cavalerie*, (A Cavalry Officer) 1905, p. 256: "'Remember well, always this' and he immobilized my hand under the pressure of his own. 'Never this' and he brought my hand to my chest." And Baucher added, "It is there that is found the secret that alone permits one to master the horse's mouth, be it outdoors or in *Haute École*, that is to say to obtain the relative lightness that suffices to hold the runaway horse, or the nearly complete lightness that in the work of *Haute École* puts the horse at the disposition of the rider (the hand acts without taking away from the impulsion)."

One could also conceive of the reduction of Baucher's principle only to its second part: legs without hand. It is this ideal that the best Portuguese bullfighting riders look to achieve, like the great João Nuncio, for example. He obtains the *rassembler* using his legs, which lightens his horses' forehand to the maximum possible and allows them the greatest mobility. His bridle hand acts only by slight indications, as witness the photographs taken at the moment when, leaving the horse all the liberty needed to elude the charge of the bull, he plants the *banderilla* in the bull's neck.

Any one of these ways of working can bring the School rider to do without aids on a horse "made" according to the spirit of dressage in the French tradition.

DIAGONAL AIDS AND LATERAL AIDS

It is patently obvious that Baucher used the *effet d'ensemble* in all periods of the evolution of his procedures. By what means did he obtain it?

Early Baucherism considered *diagonal effects* to be the most rational way to use the aids. Captain Raabe explained, in his study on locomotion, that the horse moves himself while associating his diagonal bases in each gait. And Raabe used the *diagonal effects* to control the gaits. He used these effects alternatively to get to the *effet d'ensemble*; that is to say, that he divided the opposition that the hand should make to the leg into two diagonal aids. That is what made Daudel define the *effet d'ensemble* as "the result of the use of two diagonal effects." (*Méthode d'Équitation et de Dressage*, 1857, p. 204.)

To better comprehend the procedure described by Raabe, student of Baucher that best explained the teaching of the First Manner, it is appropriate to refer to the progression that he described to get to the *diagonal effect*, for example to obtain the reverse pirouettes (turns around the forehand):

1. Leg and rein on the same side, the left for example, if one needs to move the haunches from left to right, which he calls "lateral opposition of the shoulders to the haunches;"

2. Leg only to obtain the same rotation;

3. Bridoon rein on the side opposite the leg, which he called "diagonal opposition of the shoulder to the haunches."

By following this progression, Raabe came to the use of the *diagonal effect*, which he considered the most logical. He said of the *diagonal effect* (Decarpentry, *L'Essentiel de la Méthode de Haute École de Raabe*, 1957, p. 121) that he "lightened, isolated, activated the diagonal pair on the same side, while loading, containing, and holding the opposite pair."

Another way to arrive at the *effet d'ensemble* and to school the horse is to use the *lateral aids*, recommended by the Baucherism of the later years. I think that the best explanation given for the *lateral effects*' use is found in *Questions Équestres* (1906) by General L'Hotte (pp. 66.). We learn that the rider's legs can act in two ways:

1. By pressure in place, to provoke the engagement of the hind leg under the body, and to bend the body on the side where the leg is acting (around the leg);

2. By acting backward, but without moving the leg, to make the haunches deviate.

Equipped with these two leg effects, the rider combines their use with the hand on the same side, to act on the horse with *lateral effects*. The ideal is to direct and control the horse with *lateral effects* on the side toward which he is moving or the hand on which he is working, that is to say with *direct lateral aids* (for half- passes and flying changes for instance).

L'Hotte (*Loc. cit.*, p. 95) condemns *diagonal actions* that make the horse crooked (in a sort of travers position) that ruin the proper placement of the haunches, and he only accepts these actions "as one of a number of means employed momentarily to control the *ressorts* ("springs" as in the joints of the horse) and arrive at the right position." One could respond that the *diagonal effects* are not used at the beginning, but only at the end of a progression that begins with the *lateral effects*. L'Hotte wrote: (*Loc. cit.*, p. 95) "If the haunches or the shoulders refuse to move to the right, the right rein in the first case, the left heel, in the second, gives a point of support to the resistance, supporting the opposition, be it of the shoulders to the haunches, or of the haunches to the shoulders." One could respond that the horse was not yet ready to accept *diagonal actions*. Moreover, there is a procedure that has not been accorded sufficient attention. It is the *counter diagonal action*. If the *direct diagonal action* makes the horse crooked, it needs to be compensated for by the *counter diagonal action*.

One could also criticize the *lateral effects* saying that they put the horse crooked if the leg is improperly applied. If, for example, the leg acts by pressure behind the girth, the *lateral effect*, instead of producing "the inclination" (the bend) on the side where the pressure is exerted, a travers or crookedness would result.

The rider, by means of the reins and legs, controls respectively the forelegs and the hind legs of the horse. To keep him straight, the rider must act with his hand and his two legs even if there is a predominance of certain aids over others. Some say that the combination of superior and inferior aids must be used laterally, others that the combination must be diagonal. Regardless, in the end what is important is that "the inclination" that the horse takes on from a combined action of the legs and hand (of the same side or of opposite sides) should be corrected by the contrary intervention so as always to be able to re-straighten the horse.

The rider, occupied with placing the head, with making the legs cross, assuring the relaxation of the jaw, the flexibility of the back, the cadenced impulsion of the horse, must have as his dominant preoccupation keeping the horse straight in the *corridor of the aids*, without having to worry about knowing whether he should use the *diagonal* or the *lateral aids*.

PLACING THE HORSE IN POSITION

The combination of aids that we have been discussing is important in the maintenance of a straight horse. This essential principle (keeping the horse straight) merits some comments.

One of the rules of old academic dressage was that the made horse must travel with a slight *pli* (bend) to the side of the hand on which he is working. Today there still remain traces of this rule from the *écuyers* of the XVIII century. For example, Jousseaume advises, in the canter work, to use an eighth of a lateral flexion, even on the straight. It is clear that the straighter the horse is on straight lines, the better he will adjust to the curve of the circles that a rider would make him describe. The horse must look in the direction that he is following, in half-pass and on the curves, he must be bent to the degree desired and the bend must be correct.

There is a particular case that, on this subject of lateral placement, merits the greatest attention. It applies to the counter-canter on the circle. Let us suppose a horse cantering on the right lead and describing a circle on the left hand. What is the correct lateral placement? I think that the position of the canter (to the right) should be sacrificed to that of the figure described (circle on the left hand).[42]

---

[42] Cf. General Decarpentry (*Équitation Academique*, 1949, p. 248) who advocated "*adjustment*" ("fitting") of the horse to the curve that he is describing, even if it becomes necessary to momentarily force the flexion of the horse on the side opposite the lead on which he is cantering, to get the horse to finally accept conforming himself to the curve without the intervention of the aids. (N.F.T.)

Diogo de Bragança riding Rijo. Piaffe in descent of the hand.

How to maintain the horse in this position? In the example of the horse cantering on the right lead while tracking left, the rider, if he has taught the horse to respond to diagonal actions, acts logically in using the right leg at the girth to maintain the impulsion, the left rein keeping the horse adjusted to the curve on which he is traveling. There is the application of the *diagonal effects* that Raabe practiced. For example, to make a halt on one or the other diagonal, the horse at the walk, trot, or canter, he used the *counter diagonal effect*. Inversely, "to depart at the walk, trot, or canter, on one or the other diagonal, he used the direct diagonal effect." (Decarpentry, *L'Essentiel de la Méthode de Haute École de Raabe*, 1957, p. 125)

THE SPURS

Since the spurs represent "the action of the legs progressively pushed to their greatest power" (*Loc. cit.*, p. 56), it is recommended that they be used in the *effet d'ensemble*, or in the action of the legs without opposition by the hand. Their use, which is necessary, requires much attention to detail. In effect, if the rider does not use them, he will not achieve dressage. If he uses them without method, he is headed to certain failure. He must carefully make sure of the progression with which he uses spurs if he wants to make them the most efficacious means of domination. It was because some riders did not take into account the required progression in the use of the spurs, as specified by Baucher in his First Manner, that this method of use was so severely criticized. Baucher went on to delete the use of the "*attaques*" from his later editions. However their use as an irreplaceable instrument of domination survived. With respect to the progression that Raabe recommended for the use of the spurs, the dangers that are attributed to it practically cease to exist, because Raabe gave a very extended sense to the term "*attaques*", spreading all the way from the simple menace of the calf to a stroke, even a violent one, of the spurs.

We cannot neglect the importance of the use of the spurs according to Raabe. This rider acquired such virtuosity in the use of the spurs that he expected the following effects (*Loc. cit.*, p. 56): "$1°$ They create impulsion; $2°$ they revive the horse's action; $3°$ they make him grow in his movement." They also serve to discipline him, to put him in *ramener*, to cadence him, to put him in *rassembler*, and to immobilize him.

Despite all the dangers that the spurs can present, their use – their *rational* use indeed – is indispensable. A rider cannot put aside an extended study of their effects, under threat of not achieving the proper training of a horse, even if he is working a very gifted animal. Someone has said, not without good reason: "For a good horse, a good pair of spurs is required."

Once more the criticism of Baucherism on this point is born of the results arrived at by those who have only read the writings of the master without ever seeing him work or who did not assimilate his teaching directly. They then accused the spurs of making the horses reluctant to go forward, without perceiving that the bad results come only from the lack of skill or from excessive use by the riders. Let us recall what Eugène Caron, witness to the experiment of the Baucher method at Saumur in 1842, said: "At the School, all the riders had blood on their spurs. Meanwhile in Paris, at M. Baucher's lessons, no one saw a drop." (Decarpentry, *Baucher et son École*, 1948, p. 152. [*Baucher and His School*, Xenophon Press 2011])

One of the disciples of the first phase, Gerhardt, counseled that after the flexions, the horse should be "pushed energetically to maximum speed at the canter as soon as possible after the depart from the halt," an exercise in which we see the most differentiated application of the action "legs without hand." In other respects, the *effet d'ensemble* on the spur and the *ramener outré* are capital exercises in the Second Manner that greatly accentuate the use of the spur in dressage by the Baucher method.

GENERAL ACTIONS AND PARTIAL ACTIONS

We have seen that Baucher did not use the techniques of the Old School, having understood that they were not adequate for the horsemanship of his era.

He could not think of making a Thoroughbred horse sit on his haunches by putting him in the pillars. He would need to dominate the horse, but to do so he could only fall back on the unequaled tact that inspired in him the necessary techniques.

Nevertheless we should ask whether after the invention of modern horsemanship by Baucher, there did not remain Old School techniques that had enough merit to be kept and applied; and whether Baucher himself did not use them.

It is regarding the use of *general actions* that this problem presents, as I see it, the most interest. We know that the Old School used *general actions*, and that Baucher rejected them, preferring *partial actions*, because according to him, it was easier to combat resistances one by one. One might conclude that someone who uses *general actions* does not practice Baucherism. Is that really true?

Certainly not. Because, for example, is not the *effet d'ensemble* of the First Manner a general action? Does it not have as a goal to engage the hind legs, to gymnasticize the back, to relax the jaw, to obtain the *ramener*?

On the other hand, Baucher hardly appreciated the shoulder-in, in spite of being an excellent general action. Not that he did positively condemn the exercise; but he criticized the fact that it allowed the horse to resist by "the point of support that his hind legs encounter on the wall." (*Œurves completes*, 13ᵉ éd., 1867, p. 467.) He preferred the steps to the side (lateral movements, here starting with leg-yield followed by half-pass, travers, renvers) requested very progressively (one step, then two, followed by three, etc.) and as soon as the horse gave them without resistance, he placed the head toward the side to which he was moving (*Loc. cit.*, pp. 468 and 112 – 114.)

And what about the rein-back? This exercise, when it is not executed with correction, which is almost always the case in the beginning of training, does not work the loins much, nor the hindquarters. It is hardly then but a local action. But later, when the movement is well diagonalized, and the horse is in hand and light, the rein-back becomes a general action. This permits us to confirm that Baucher had recourse to *general actions*. This observation is very important, because Baucher considered the rein-back as an essential exercise and practiced it a great deal. At the beginning of his career, it is said, he made his horses rein-back 100 steps, while he only went forward 10 steps.

There are finally the famous *attaques* of the spur on a fixed hand, with the horse in place. Isn't this a clear example of a general action used by the Baucherist system?

It was logical that Baucher would start with *partial actions*. It is well known for example, that no horse would consent straightaway to the *effet d'ensemble* in place or even to regular rein-back. It was after having exercised the different parts of the horse (in the *partial actions*) that Baucher started the *general actions*. That was when he worked together the muscles and joints that he had previously and separately gymnasticized. So it is only after having practiced the flexion of the jaw and the neck, the pirouettes and reverse pirouettes (turns on the forehand), which are *partial actions*, that the rein-back, a general action, is undertaken.

RESISTANCES OF WEIGHT AND FORCE

How must the rider combat the resistances of weight and the resistances of force? By *general actions*, or by *partial actions*?

It is known that the first of these resistances are connected to general equilibrium, the second come from muscular contractions. For the problem of resistances of weight, it seems that the question does not arise. Even if we wanted, we could not combat them by means of *partial actions*. Every action used (Baucher used half-halts) to shift an excess of weight from the forehand to the hindquarters has an inevitable effect on the horse's balance. From that fact alone, the half-halt can only be considered to be a general action.

On the contrary, muscular contractions can be approached directly: vibrations, little *attaques* of the legs. These are *partial actions*.

GENERAL AND PARTIAL ACTIONS USED SIMULTANEOUSLY

Analyzing in more detail the problem that is concerning us, we can come to the conclusion that Baucher used *general* and *partial actions* at the same time.

In the changes of direction, the voltes, the work on two tracks, one can use the outside rein to direct the horse – a general action, and also vibrations on the inside rein to maintain the relaxation of the jaw – a *partial action*. For the *ramener* to be correct, the participation of the jaw, the poll, and the neck are required, and for the *ramener* to be maintained, the participation of the horse's back and legs is also needed.

The question of *general* and *partial actions* discussed above has been little discussed in equestrian literature, and we believe that this is the first time that their simultaneous use by Baucher has been brought to light. This clarification results from correspondence on the subject exchanged between Viscount de Paço de Nespereira and the author.

BAUCHER'S TWO MANNERS

The comparison of Baucher's two manners (the first from Baucher himself, and tempered by Wachter, Gerhardt, and Raabe; the second definitively explained by L'Hotte, Faverot, and Beudant) allows us to arrive at the following conclusions.

At the end of dressage, the horse's forehead must, save some exceptions, be near and slightly in front of the vertical.

Just as the lowered neck is a preparatory position in the First Manner, the elevation of the neck, in which the head can be raised to approach the horizontal, is a preparatory position in the Second Manner.

The progression of the Second Manner is without a doubt more kind, but when it is used to bring the horse into an academic dressage balance, it uses methods of domination comparable to those of the First Manner (Faverot, *Dressage Méthodique du Cheval de Selle...,* 1891, Part Four: "Fixer." *Methodical Dressage of the Riding Horse*, Xenophon Press 2010, Part Four: "Confirming the Horse's Position"), methods that had been rejected as too restrictive. In addition, early Baucherism employed the "attacks." In the Baucherism of the Second Manner, they are prescribed in the same way.

Early Baucherism used the *effet d'ensemble* according to the original principle; Baucherism of the Second Manner comes back to using it after the use of the hand without the legs, and legs without the hand.

Baucher himself explained the evolution from one manner to the other (from the First Manner to the Second Manner) in the Preface to the 12th edition of his complete works: "This twelfth edition is distinguished from those preceding it in that I have corrected those passages that seemed to me incomplete, and taken out those that, through experience, I have found to be of little use, replacing them with other techniques that are simpler and more effective. It also differs in that I have introduced some new principles that perfect the education of the horse."

"With my method, one can give every horse a balance of a second and a third class. And the twenty-six horses that I have ridden in public have been incontestable proof that, with my new principles, I am presenting not only an easy means to obtain these two classes of balance with all horses, and the infallible means to obtain in any horse constant lightness, the sign of perfect balance. It is this balance that I call first class."

"The first two classes of balance suffice for all the needs of the cavalry and ordinary horsemanship."

"Perfect equilibrium or balance of the first class can only be given to a horse by *élite* riders. It will be transcendental equitation. In poetry, in the arts, in the sciences, not everyone can go to Corinth!" (This Greek proverb means that not all people can achieve the most sophisticated goals, due to a lack of ability.)

GINETA, BAUCHER, AND BULLFIGHTING

The duel in bullfighting on horseback is certainly **an expression, much more refined**, of the old way of riding *à la Gineta*. Compared to the pure *Gineta*, the stirrups are longer, the bits much less harsh, and regular spurs are substituted for the sort of daggers in use during the historical period. Even if the duel is no longer between two men, but between the *genet* (jennet) (that is to say the couple formed by the horse and the *Gineta* rider) and the bull, the spectacle of the horse launched at the gallop, stopping instantly, reining back, and executing rapid pirouettes, is directly inspired by *la Gineta* horsemanship.

The great Tauromachic rider (bullfighter), João Nuncio explains to us, "The rider must dominate his horse, but dominate him totally, in a fashion that, if the horse is afraid, he respects his rider more than he worries about his fear of the bull." Moreover, "When the horse is well subjugated, he becomes a handy instrument for his rider; he does not have his own will anymore, he does what he is ordered to do."

When the horse is well-trained, the bit has no purpose anymore because the rider commands the horse with his legs, which "play like on a piano" on the flanks of the horse. The same touches produce the same sounds, meaning that the rider's legs must always transmit the same orders. It is Baucher's principle: legs without hand. The aids are used alternatively during the training. At the end of dressage, the rider's hands or his legs prevail as the main aid according to his tact and the horsemanship that he has chosen.

Diamantino Viseu, "*diestro*"(master) of the "*corrida*" on foot, stated, *à propos* of João Nuncio at his hundredth birthday in 2001, "The jennets who practice Tauromachic horsemanship in Portugal are connected across time in its age-old practice."

It is at the walk and the gallop that one fights, hunts, or practices Tauromachic horsemanship.

Nuncio applied the procedures of the Second Manner of Baucher's methods, which I consider, in various aspects to be a moderate form of Gineta horsemanship, very different from the *Doma vaquera* (reining and stock riding) that is practiced in Spain and is related to Moorish horsemanship.

In support of this opinion, I cite Baucher: "Quick as lightening, the horse launches forward; he stops, immobile as a crossed bayonet; he seems to flee, and by a thousand detours, wants to escape whatever pursues him; but for the rapid half-turns, he comes back on his haunches, changes lead, turns tightly, circles, jumps hedges and fences!" (*Œuvres completes*, 13^e edition, 1867, page 621). The master had those words for the trained saddle horse and the cavalry officer of his era.

This kind of balance describes the goal to attain from the dressage of a horse that is destined to bullfighting on horseback.

The horsemanship of *Gineta* and Baucher have the same purpose and are practiced on the same horses. But the Master got there by methods that were more rational, kind, and progressive.

Baucherism appeared for the training of thoroughbred horses and crossbreds from the thoroughbred. In our day, the *Doma vaquera* and the *Gineta* are practiced similarly on horses resulting from crosses between Andalusians, Arabs, and Thoroughbreds, called *los très sangres* (the three bloods). The horsemanship initially practiced by Baucher became an artistic form of dressage with his exhibitions presented at the circus in the same way that the horsemanship of João Nuncio has become artistic, practiced in the bullfighting arena.

The risk for me, in advancing such ideas, is to be killed by the pundits of horsemanship.

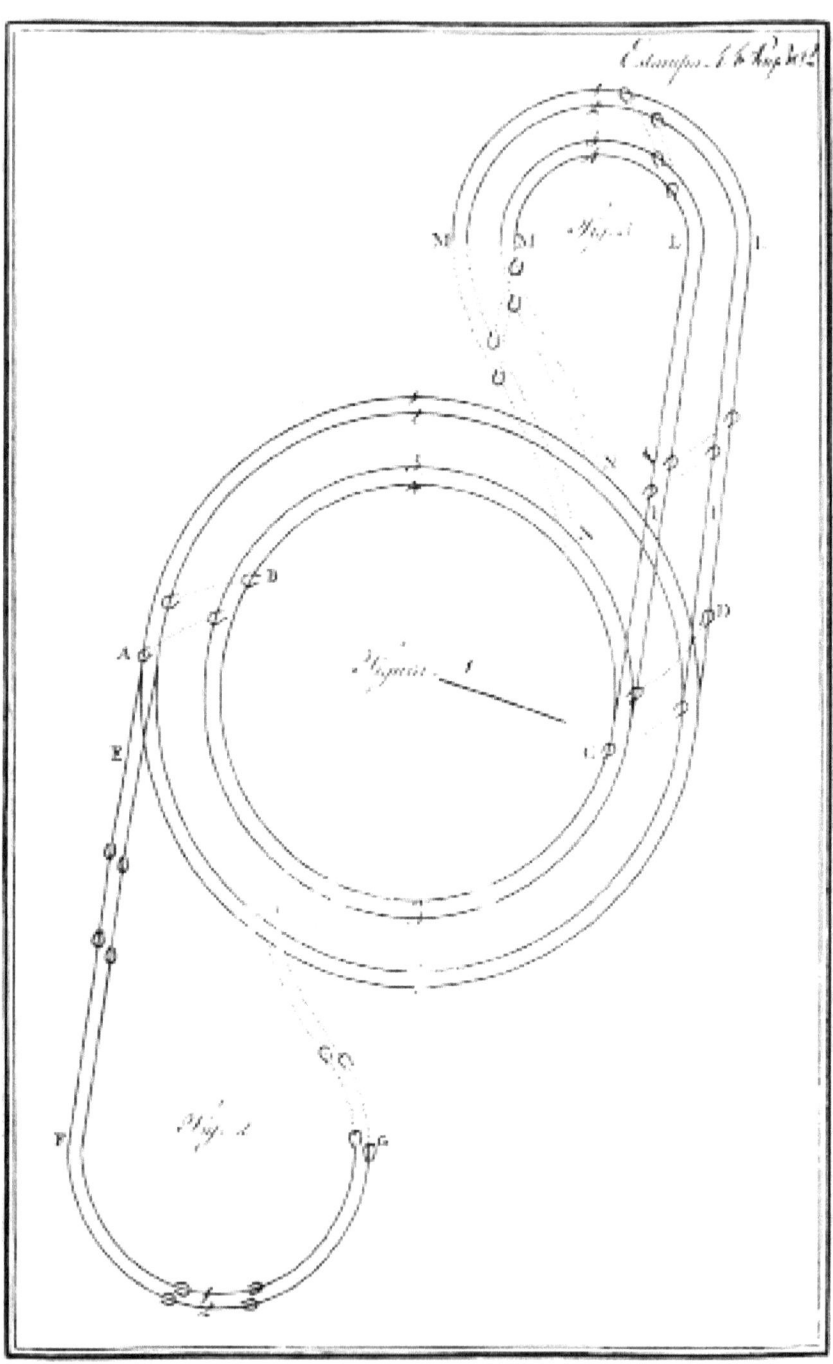

Reverse volte to the left, Volte to the left and demi-volte.

PART THREE

CURRENT OVERVIEW OF ACADEMIC HORSEMANSHIP

After having made an examination of the two great horsemanship systems of ancient times, and more recently, let us now observe what seem to be of the contemporary concepts in the matter of "dressage." We can also make an evaluation of what remains of academic dressage today.

Even in the era of the Royal Academies, the golden age of which was the XVIII century, we see appear, aside from School Horsemanship, a military equitation of whom the father was, in France, Colonel d'Auvergne. His goal was to simplify the methods from academic horsemanship.

Today, having been replaced by multiple types of mechanical equipment, the horse has nearly completely disappeared from most military organizations. Some people find that the horse should not be entirely banished. The practice of horsemanship has given birth to and developed the rider spirit: "required to dominate at any moment a living will that has abrupt and changing reactions, that gives to the most humble rider audacity, flexibility, a sharp eye, rapid decisiveness, and disregard for danger" (Decarpentry, *Les Maîtres Écuyers du Manège de Saumur*, 1954. Introduction by General du Breuil, former Commandant of the Cavalry School).

The horse has disappeared from the field of battle, but there is no doubt that it would be good to maintain the rider spirit. It has been many years since General Weygand wrote, "Whatever the evolution that the future reserves for it, there will always be a cavalry, that is to say an arm more rapid than the rest of the corps, whose role will be reconnaissance, maneuver, and pursuit, that carried by horse or steel, will find success in the audacity, speed, and surprise that will be, in a word, the proof of the rider spirit, with all that this spirit must comport in decision, loyalty, elegance, performance, and morale, and the taste for risk, too." The cavalry has changed away from horses, but its spirit must survive.

Military equitation has taken its own road, separating itself from School horsemanship. For many reasons, *écuyers*, left out of the academies that had closed their doors, emigrated to various civilian *manèges*, sometimes to the circus, even to a military school like Saumur[43] or a civilian one like the Spanish Riding School of Vienna.

In the end, the interest aroused by the method that Baucher brought to the world of riding has not lasted. *Haute École* has finished by being discredited now that people no longer have need of the horse to move around or they have used it for other ends.

The Portuguese rider rides, still a little at least, with the care to have a "made" horse, first because by temperament, he loves to have a handy mount, and besides, because mounted bullfighting, born in Portugal, and still honored there, requires a special preparation founded on academic dressage. This national spectacle maintains enthusiasm among the few who still today ride horses that are really trained.

Haute École has, under somewhat different forms, for the ultimate refuge: the dressage competitions that follow the programs of the *Fédération Équestre Internationale* (FEI), the presentations at the circus and in the equestrian theaters– where some *écuyers* still work honorably; that is, if they have the tact and time required to not have recourse to non-equestrian techniques, the use of horses by bullfighting riders, the teaching of a master in a few rare *manèges*, and the work of amateurs that still dedicate themselves to this superior form of the use of the saddle horse.

---

43 Of which the "civilianization" has had it operate under the name *École Nationale d'équitation.* (N.F.T.)

[This page intentionally left blank]

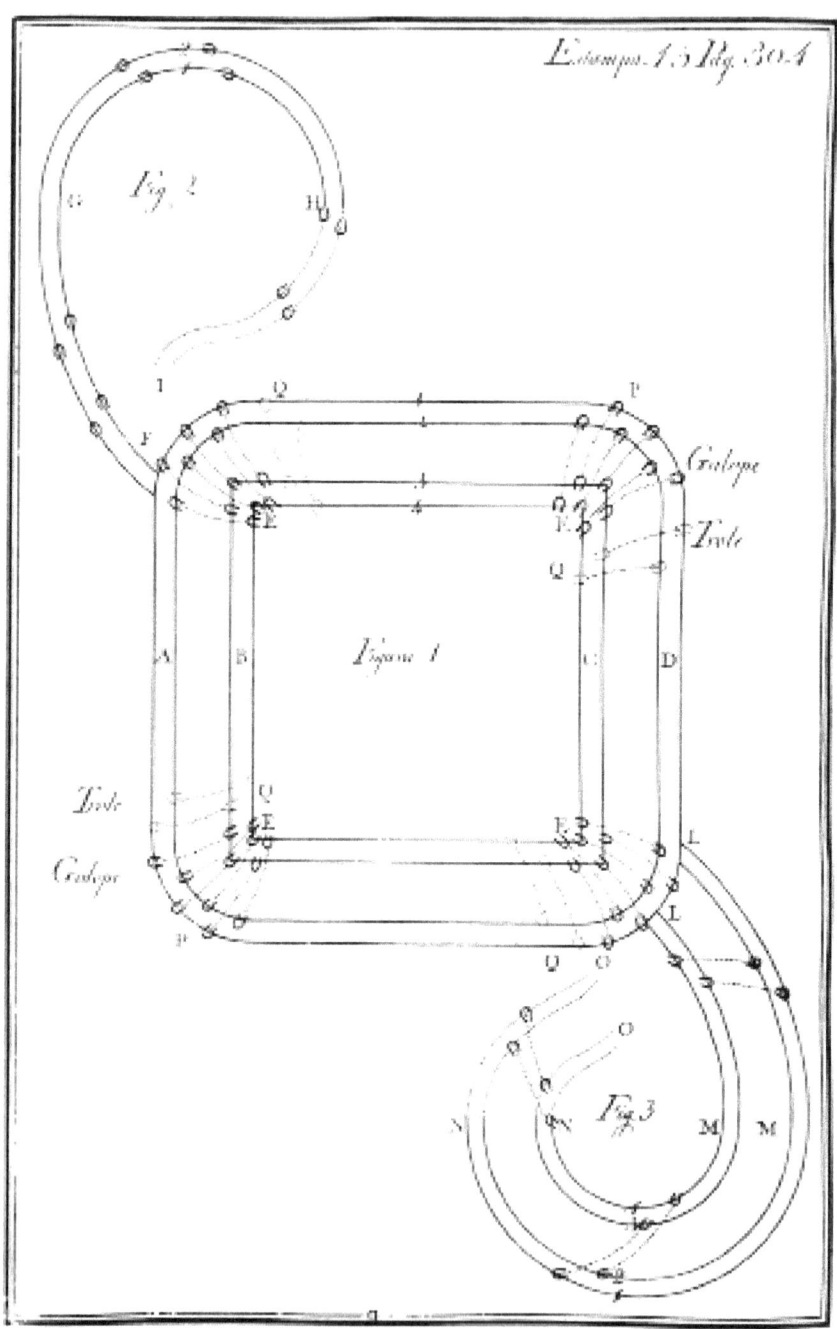

Square volte to the right and change of hand.

CHAPTER 1

ACADEMIC HORSEMANSHIP IN FÉDÉRATION ÉQUESTRE INTERNATIONALE PROGRAMS

The "dressage" tests that take place today under the auspices of the FEI, with the support of the equestrian federations of the member countries, are set out in defined programs that "are of graduated difficulty divided in classes, corresponding to the stage of training of the horses for which they are intended." (Decarpentry, *Équitation Académique*, 1949, p.20.)

So of the dressage tests provided, the most simple – those of the Three Day Event – require that, having to conquer in one part, the tough requirements of the cross-country course over fixed obstacles, and in another part, those of a course of stadium jumping, the horse knows the rudimentary aids and how to execute the lateral and longitudinal movements that gymnasticize him. He must be at his ease in the horizontal balance that puts him in the best condition to complete a severe cross-country course and to tackle the steeplechase at the desired speed.

The Prix Saint Georges and the more complicated Intermediaire tests, call for a superior degree of dressage, not only through the difficulty of the exercises required, but also through the submission that the horse must demonstrate.

In the Grand Prix de Dressage, the problems of academic dressage are approached. It is very difficult, and the test can only be met by a horse specialized in this work.

Even if, as we have seen, the first of these four tests demands a horizontal balance with a relatively extended base of support, we must realize that this balance will only be good in the measure that the contact (*appui*) in the hand will be light. That is a necessary condition for a good journey through uneven terrain strewn with obstacles.

In the other more difficult tests, the exercises and airs must demonstrate the merits of the competitors. The marks given out by the judges are established according to criteria that call for certain observations about the performance.

These marks can be technically criticized for three principal reasons:

1. The preference given to horses having naturally ample gaits;

2. Attribution of the same coefficients to exercises that are of very different difficulty;

3. The preponderance given to the precision of an exercise to the detriment of its beauty.

One could add to these criticisms the observation often made that, in any international jury, a judge might assign the highest scores to his compatriots. And that "there are judges that systematically classify badly the competitors from certain countries." (Major Reymão Nogueira, *Ano Hipico Portugues*, 1956–1957.)

THE PREFERENCE GIVEN TO HORSES

WITH NATURALLY AMPLE GAITS

It is understandable that horses would be chosen as a function of the natural beauty of their free and ample gaits characteristic of the blood horses of our time, with a rectangular (long and slender) conformation. On the other hand, this longer lined conformation creates some issues. Because of this conformation, the execution of very collected airs becomes in effect much more difficult for blood horses than for horses of other breeds, in particular those of Iberio-Lusitano breeding.

The Baron de Grovesthius wrote in the review *Ano Hipico Portugues* (1956 -1957), "A test in the 'Grand Prix de Dressage' at the Olympic Games is a work of art that does not depend only on the rider. It is an ensemble in which different elements are concurrent: the beauty and gaits of the horse, and the presentation that the rider makes with his personal talent."

Where is the beauty in the passage and piaffe of the majority of the blood horses that are presented? They can be more or less correctly practiced, but they never have, or almost never, the majesty of those of good peninsular horses.

The Andalusian has naturally more brilliance. His movement comes from certain physical dispositions. His neck is often stronger and relatively shorter as he is generally kept a stud. On this subject, General L'Hotte noted (*Questions Équestres*, 1906, p. 117) "that a long neck, although it is light, puts more weight on the shoulders than a thick but short neck, and that its changes of position entrain changes of weight that are far more perceptible (than those of a short neck)."

The Russian riders who participated at the *Concours hippique international* (today CSI) in Paris in 1959 had stallions that made a great impression by the facility with which they were jumped. An article by Colonel des Roches de Chassay appearing in the review *L'Année Hippique* (1959 – 1960) underlined this fact. He arrived at the conclusion that the conformation most favorable to a jumping horse is that of an animal with a short neck and a long loin, a conformation that approaches that of the feline, jumper *par excellence* among the quadrupeds.

The author of the article reported on the opinion of a trainer of trotting horses: "If there were no neck, if we could remove that and stick the head onto the shoulders, how much more simple would our trade be." He reported also on the opinion of an *écuyer*, who notably he did not identify: "In dressage... it is always the damned necks that bring up the biggest problems." And Colonel des Roches added:

"... One searches for long loins, a desirable quality, bringing suppleness. But, hell! A long loin is almost always accompanied by a long neck. One finds rarely, if not ever, one without the other.

"So it is a question of knowing if one wants to profit from a long loin, and suffer a front end that is a hindrance, or better to prefer a short neck, and have the disadvantage of a short back. Between two evils, choose the last. For stadium jumping, I still prefer the second formula."

All these considerations re-enforce our defense of horses from the Iberian Peninsula. We believe that the breed is maintained because it possesses the qualities that bullfighting riders look for. These horses have powerful short necks. Even when their backs are weak, they are very handy, as one could acknowledge from the rapidity with which they move from side to side when, in the arena, they want to meet the bull, or to evade him....

I do not conclude that the Iberian horses should be preferred for dressage tests. I want to emphasize that the good peninsular horse, sadly rare but still in existence, brings to certain airs a beauty and a majesty that one does not find in horses of other breeds.

It is for no other reason that, up to the beginning of the XIX century, the peninsular horse had been considered the best for academic dressage. We know horses of this breed that, aside from their natural disposition to the *rassembler* are "forward" as they say, and who, even if they do not have movement with extraordinary natural amplitude, display nonetheless, gaits that are extended enough and move with extreme elegance. It would be worth the trouble to envisage the use of this horse for international dressage competition. At the 1972 Olympics, were there not a great diversity of types of horses presented?

SAME COEFFICIENT FOR EXERCISES
OF DIFFERENT DIFFICULTY

The score of each competitor is made up of the average from disparate criteria that combined with the nationalism of each of the members of the jury, leads to altogether unbelievable results. "At the Olympic Games of 1956, a rider was placed first by the judge at A, and ninth by the judge at B. Another was placed fifteenth by the judge at A, and second by the judge at B." (*Ano Hipico Portugues*, 1956 – 1957)

Another aspect of dressage judging that is absolutely unacceptable is to attribute the same coefficient to exercises of manifestly different difficulty, for example, for the transition from the collected trot to the lengthened trot, and the transition from piaffe to passage. At these same Olympic Games in 1956, a particular special value had been given to passage and to piaffe, but at the last moment, the deletion of coefficients removed this advantage... for these who had obtained it. (*Ano Hipico Portugues*, 1956 – 1957, p. 40)

For "natural" that could be the last two airs mentioned; the rider who has taught them knows well the difficulties encountered, and knows that they do not compare in any way to those of the lengthening of the trot.

A transition from piaffe to passage and vice versa depends above all on the skill of the rider, while the lengthening and collecting of the three gaits only reflect the blood, the breed, and the balance of the horse, in a way that it is on the horse that it most depends.

To give the same coefficient to an air obtained by the skill of the rider as to another air that depends almost exclusively on the horse is to put the man on the same level as the horse. It does not take into account the tact and intelligence that the rider has shown. If they continue to score the tests this way, I maintain that the riders should not accept their prizes. Logically, they should give the rewards that have been credited to them... to the breeders of their mounts.

A similar view was expressed by Commandant Licart in *L'Éperon* of February 1956: "The dressage tests are neither examinations of horsemanship nor model presentations" (where judges look at the horses' natural gaits). Showing, moreover, that he well recognized the influence of certain members of the jury over others, which leads to subversion of the final results, Commandant Licart did not hesitate to recommend that each judge be isolated, and flanked by a secretary, so that his attention would never be deficient. After each contestant's test, the forms should be collected by the secretary, who would then do the math necessary to the ranking.

GREATER IMPORTANCE GIVEN TO THE PRECISION
OF AN EXERCISE TO THE DETRIMENT OF ITS BEAUTY

It has been noted, about of the characteristics of the dressage tests of today, that exactitude – the primary occupation of the German School – has been preferred to the beauty that has been the primary preoccupation of the French School, even if that beauty was not accompanied by a perfect precision in the obedience to the aids. The question goes back a long way, and great riders have compared the German and French Schools, ever since Baucherism provoked a schism from the Old School doctrine that had been followed unanimously and without great differences of interpretation, by all of the European equestrian academies.

The German School, which has always applied the teaching of the Old French School with a view to obtaining great precision in the movements, was in open war with the Baucherism that was presenting a new method to explore every horse's possibilities. The Old School in France accorded great value to brilliance in equestrian art. Baucher's techniques, which produced even more brilliance, delivered a severe blow to the Old School. And while France boasted of having one more great *écuyer*, it was mainly Germany that took to heart the defense of the old manner.

Witness the pamphlet published by the German Louis Seeger in Berlin, in 1853. His *Sérieux Avertissement aux Cavaliers d'Allemagne* (*Serious Warning to German Riders*), French translation, excerpts in Appendix to Decarpentry, *Baucher et son École*, Paris, 1987 [Appendix II to Decarpentry, *Baucher and His School*, Xenophon Press 2011]put German riders on guard against the propaganda of Baucher's method. Seeger sought to reduce the value of Baucherism to nothing by contrasting it to the advantages of the old method.

One cannot say that Seeger supported his critique on very plausible arguments, even though in the middle of the XIX century, he was one of the most renowned German *écuyers*.

For reasons not well known, Baucher's presentations in Berlin were made on very mediocre horses. But in justification, 'Blacknick' or 'Rufus' which could not have the elegance and brilliance of a fine horse, proved that their lack of blood and their defective conformation did not impede them from executing the most difficult airs.

"Lesson of the rassembler."
Preparation for the canter by the passage and piaffe."
Aubert, 1836.

Seeger's criticism dates from 1853. Baucherism, at that time, had not attained the maturity that would lead it to the Second Manner. Seeger, concerned with showing that his method was the better of the two, described himself to be the successor to La Guérinière, however he applied those techniques with his Germanic temperament, and thus greatly modified the horsemanship that he claimed to represent.

Technically, here are the criticisms that Seeger addressed to Baucher:

Horizontal balance can only serve for everyday dressage, not for *Haute École*.

Baucher's rassembler required the horse to bring his four legs together, which often put him on his shoulders instead of making him flex from the haunches to the stifles.

The trot is heavy, and in piaffe, the hind legs escape laterally instead of advancing under the body, while the forelegs do not lift sufficiently.

At the canter, the horse carries himself alternately on the forehand and on the hindquarters "in a movement that presents a certain analogy to that of a wave."

Finally after even many more criticisms, Seeger finished by

The horse, in the position of a mountain goat on a peak,
One of the positions practiced in early Baucherism...finds in the piaffe the correction of the gait.

"...The four reins in the left hand, the right hand posed on both of the right reins."
Aubert, 1836.

treating Baucher as a charlatan, and called him the *"gravedigger of French dressage."*

Of the criticisms made of the German School by the French, we will select those of Baron de Vaux (*Écuyers et Écuyères*, 1893, p. 179). Comparing horses trained in the German manner with those according to the French School, he wrote, "The first (German), instead of coming out light and suppled, of flowing between the hands and legs of his rider like the second (French), comes off the ground ponderously, so that he seems to leave the movement that he is already performing with regret and effort. The 'crushing[44]' because one cannot give the name 'suppling' to this fashion of using the aids, operates by throwing the weight onto the hindquarters where it remains fixed. But this part of the horse's body... from which emanates all the impulsion that the forehand is destined to receive and continue by forward projection, finds itself partially paralyzed. 'Squashed' instead of being 'lightened,' as in the French School, it is necessary therefore for the croup to contract its muscles with great effort in order to put the body into movement. And yet this effort, acting on 'immobility,' is necessarily hard and ungainly, because any movement in itself would not be different (in quality) from the position from which it proceeds and is the consequence."

---

44 *brisement*

The same Baron de Vaux (pp. 220 – 221) wrote about the work of Mme. Maestricht, celebrated *écuyère* in the circus:

"She proceeds according to the German School, that school that any man having the intelligence and a sentiment for the art should know not to accept in either its principle or in its execution since it accurately represents what Baron d'Etreillis called very fairly 'equestrian automatism.' This definition well characterizes this school which has as a principle to make the horse obey brusquely and mechanically under a stiff and immobile rider. From the point of view of art, this leaves a bit to be desired."

"This complete subjugation" of the mechanism of the horse could offer, honestly, in certain cases and for certain uses, more precision and straightness in the execution, but as Baron d'Etreillis said, this manner is absolutely automatic, so stripped of elegance and harmony, that it takes away from the rider all his real value, because his mount is reduced to the role of a lever under him."

After this technical analysis by Baron de Vaux, let us make the point using what General Decarpentry said on the same subject, at the beginning of his *Équitation Academic* (1949).

When the School of Horsemanship at Versailles, heir to the academies of the Renaissance, finally closed its doors for good in 1830, its teaching was supposed to be passed on at the School at Saumur. But when Comte d'Aure, though a student at the famous Academy, was named *Écuyer en chef* at Saumur, he put academic dressage to the side, and made a more practical method prevail. His method was in his view more suitable for a military school. This did not prevent him, as well as the *écuyers* that were under his orders, from practicing, individually and also in *reprises* (organized group presentations,) the School airs and jumps inspired by those of the School of Versailles.

The appearance of Baucherism started a new era in dressage.

In 1843, on the recommendation of the Cavalry Committee, Marshal Soult, Minister of War, ordered an experiment with the Baucher method to be carried out in the French Army. The method was not adopted, for reasons of rivalry, the explanation of which does not belong here, despite the most laudatory reports on the results obtained, in particular the one from Commandant Novital, then *Écuyer en chef* (Chief Rider) at Saumur, and "in spite of the advantages of the substantial

**Jardin, trained and ridden by Diogo de Bragança.
Trot with extension. Confident and bold.**

reduction in the time necessary up until then to perform the training."
(Decarpentry, *Academic Équitation,* 1949). One might think that the
failure of this trial was to the good. The troops in the ranks might have
had difficulty in assimilating the procedures that today still appear to be
dangerous in the hands of those who have insufficient tact.

So military equitation became entirely d'Aurist, meanwhile
French *Haute École*, at the end of the XIX and the beginning of the XX
centuries, came under the influence of Baucherism.

Before Baucher, horsemanship was similar in France, Portugal,
and among the Germanic people. Baucherism had practically no
following among the latter, where they continued to claim to follow La
Guérinière.

While the French School passed through the vicissitudes of a
long evolution, the School of Vienna remained practically unchanged in
its doctrine. It proclaimed its fidelity to the principles of La Guérinière,
whose work continued to be their equestrian bible. At the same time,
they were unaware of Baucher. But in fact, even if this school kept to the

Intrépido, trained and ridden by Diogo de Bragança. Piaffe. High in the withers and neck, calm and majestic.

teaching of an *écuyer* that was not one of their own, the application of his procedures were subjected to alterations due to ethnic differences.

Without descending into brutality, the riders at the Vienna School voluntarily persist in direct opposition to the horse's resistances, instead of applying themselves to negating[45] the resistances (Baucherism).

They demand "the unconditional capitulation of the horse more than seeking his generous participation in the realization of cooperative work." (*Loc. cit.*) They attach "more value to a rigorous exactitude in the execution than in the joyous ease of their mount in his bearing and the scope of his movement." (*Loc. cit.*) "For lack of looking outward, of instructive comparisons, and especially of emulation, the Germanic school became a little numb in the admiration of the results, admittedly incontestable, that they obtained." (*Loc. cit.*)

At the beginning of the XX century, the French and German schools were ignorant of each other. It is to the honor of the FEI to have

---

45 *dissociation*

put them in front of one another, by instituting their meeting in periodic competitions. At first, their styles appeared to be in complete opposition to each other.

The riders of "the Romantic School," as the French School was called on the other side of the Rhine, made a demonstration of goodwill more than exactitude and of facility more than application in the work. The French gave the impression to have in their dressage "eluded difficulties more than to have resolved them." (We continue to cite General Decarpentry). In the unfurling of the tests, they appeared a bit too casual and a bit imprecise in guiding the horse.

On their side, the riders of the German School gave the impression of having obtained exemplary submission, a bit forced, sometimes apathetic, and also "a rigorous precision, but more mechanized than animated." The results obtained demonstrated a "studious application." Nevertheless, they retained the mark "of a visibly laborious effort."

"The opinions of the judges diverged no less sharply in that they belonged to one or the other school, and established scores that provoked passionate discussions."

"But the contestants quickly learned to observe each other. Without abandoning whatever in their own manner turned to their advantage, each of them strove to combine with it whatever they approved of in the manner of their neighbor."

From year to year, the differences were a little less marked. The styles of the two schools came together, without completely merging - happily for equestrian art. There even remained some quite notable differences, as we shall see. As it concerns French horsemanship, General Decarpentry judged that since the 1930s, international dressage competition put the competitors "in front of problems so difficult to resolve" that the French military teaching "still more or less d'Aurist, proved its insufficiency for anything beyond everyday horsemanship."

EXHIBITIONS AND COMPETITIONS

It is appropriate for us to review the difference between exhibitions or presentations and competitions.

Exhibitions, whether individual or collective, have existed since there has been School horsemanship. In the past they acted to show, in times of peace, the degree of preparation for combat on horseback. From there stemmed the *passades*[46], pirouettes, *terre-à-terre*, etc., tourneys with the quintaine[47] and the races to the "heads" and to the "ring," and all the exercises that "were instituted to present an agreeable image and instruction in war." (La Guérinière, *École de Cavalerie*, 1754 [*School of Horsemanship, Part II*, Xenophon Press 1992])

With competition, the presentation ceased to have a purely spectacular character. It became a test that had the goal of showing the relative quality of the work executed by the different participants. A necessarily common program was imposed, serving as a base of comparison that permitted the ranking of the contestants.

The FEI tests belong to the category of competition and because of that have a different character from presentations – which happily still exist, such as those of the Spanish Riding School in Vienna and at the School at Saumur.

GREATER IMPORTANCE OF GERMANIC CRITERIA IN INTERNATIONAL JURIES

For reasons that are patriotic, political, yet not very much of an equine nature, the judges in the competitions have a tendency to favor that which comes closest to their concepts, even when the competitors are not just their compatriots. Actually, with the majority of judges having a Germanic equestrian education, the "beyond-the-Rhine" style predominates and the competitors take that into account. This is why Colonel Lesage, winner of the Grand Prix de Dressage at the Olympic Games in Los Angeles in 1932, wrote in *L'Éperon* in February 1957, "It is worth more to have a horse in frank contact with the hand than a horse

46 (repeated passes at the gallop down the long side with half voltes and changes of lead at each end)
47 An object mounted on a post or attached to a movable crossbar mounted on a post, used as a target in the medieval art of tilting.

susceptible of being too talkative."

When a French rider, a former *Écuyer en chef* at Saumur, speaks this way there is enough proof that the precision of the movements has become the priority in the requirements that are demanded of a trained horse, whereas before 1940, the greater criterion was that the horse knew how to use his back (M. Glahn); that is to say, that before all else, the attention was on flexibility and impulsion, and consequently on the lightness that derived from these two qualities.

Has the Germanic concept been beneficial to the progress of contemporary academic dressage?

I believe yes, as far as precision is concerned. The tests judged according to Germanic criteria require, in effect, a considerable precision in the aids. It is true that the precise execution of movements demanded is facilitated by the pressure– accepted and currently practiced – of the lower jaw on the bit. But this kind of contact (*appui*) is not indispensable. It is possible to attain precision in the movements with a horse having a light mouth. But it is more difficult.

The use of a certain contact (*appui*) has in fact facilitated the task of riders, in that they have tackled dressage tests in greater number, than if they had to ride with a light hand. Yet one could ask whether that has really been to the advantage of true academic dressage.

THE CONCEPT OF LIGHTNESS

It is without a doubt that a horsemanship imprinted with true lightness is not available to everyone. Its practice is extremely difficult especially when the lightness must be combined with great precision. It remains no less the only dressage that gives us, through the behavior of the horse, the measure of the rider's tact.

Naturally, as we have already said, when lightness ceases to constitute the principal concern of riders, the quantity of contestants in dressage tests increases and their quality diminishes. Do not forget that, even in the golden age of academic dressage, great *écuyers* were very rare. It is not in extending wine with water that one produces more good wine!

Let us look for a moment at the notion of lightness, and begin

Formoso, trained by Alfreso Conde, ridden by João Trigueiros de Aragão. Passage. "...So that the horse puts himself behind the hand, while rising in the withers and the neck, at the same time as he is in front of the leg."
General L'Hotte.

by remarking that it is connected to a number of activities. The theory of relaxation (or *decontraction* as it is called in French) recommended notably for medical and sporting purposes constitutes, as a whole nothing other than a theory of lightness transformed into a state of habit; its application allows an individual to put into action, only the muscles necessary, to produce the desired result.

Any movement that is executed using more force than is necessary cannot be pursued for long because it is fatiguing. Furthermore the employment of useless force detracts from the quality of execution.

In horsemanship, one who follows the example of the German School, considers the horse as a being that must unconditionally submit, even if it renders him glumly somnolent, and not as a partner forming a harmonious ensemble with his rider, does not put dressage on the esthetic level to which it belongs. The practice of *"l'appui"* (contact with weight or pressure), a useless effort, does not allow *"soutenir sans tenir"* (support without holding) – which corresponds to the Baucherist ideal: "Semi-tension on the reins and light touch of the pant leg."

Nobody in horsemanship produces anything of beauty if he or she does not give the impression of acting with the ease of those who do everything well that they do.

This is what the Spanish call, "the difficult made easy." Everything appears so simple that everyone is ready to believe that they could do as well. And yet, enormous preparatory work is necessary to get to the apparent suppression of effort.

In *Haute École*, the ease that we can observe in various positions results from what we technically call lightness. It is the way in which to work a horse that obeys his rider without the least reticence. He executes the movements indicated by means of aids so subtle that they become invisible. Therefore, one can understand that after a certain point, dressage takes on a personal character, as Baucher said, the connection between the horse and his rider becomes, in fact, intimate. The rider can offer himself the luxury of improvising such new airs as his imagination might dictate. When the horse achieves this degree of dressage, he does not need orders, but solicitations that are barely expressed. The horse attentively responds as if he were proud to have on his back a friend who leaves him sufficient liberty so that he can carry his rider with grace and majesty.

This is possible only with absolute lightness.

LIGHTNESS AND SUPPORTIVE CONTACT[48]

Before technically defining lightness, let us examine the larger sense of the word (lightness). General L'Hotte (*Un Officier de Cavalerie*, 1905, p. 126) wrote: "the perfection dreamed of resides, as much for the talent of the rider as for the dressage of the horse, much less in what has come to be called equestrian difficulties than in the purity of movement."

This purity rests on the rider putting into play only the forces useful to the envisioned movements, and on the use that the horse makes of those forces.

The word lightness is most often used in a restrained sense.... Then it only means the relaxation of the jaw.

In fact, the first meaning that a specific work be executed with only the forces useful to its production constitutes the goal to be attained. Horsemanship that recommends contact (pressure), as soft as it might be, of the bit with the lower jaw, not permitting the absolute free play of the jaw, obligates the horse into a useless effort. Even small, this effort exceeds that which was just necessary for the production of the requested movement. And this goes not only for the horse, but also for the rider who cannot completely relax his muscles, in that he must act against the horse so that the contact is not lost.

So it is certainly not by way of contact (*appui*) that the relaxation of the horse-rider ensemble can be realized.

Wachter wrote (*Aperçus Équestres*, 1862, p. 91): "The best support that one can give to a horse is the certain support that one teaches him to take on the ground by the extremities of his pillars of support (the legs). The hand, by itself, supports nothing. It can only alert the horse. It can without a doubt, at a given moment, cause a shift in weight that unloads a compromised pillar; but on difficult terrain, what tells you that in wanting to hold back the forehand, you would not at all crush the hindquarters? What about horses that stumble in front and fall on the rear! But the suppled horse, adroit with his legs, knows how to move them in any direction, to give them the degree of suspension and extension that each step requires. He knows, like the mountain horse, accustomed to having the reins on his neck, to make a large step, to make a small step, to take a solid hold on the ground or only skim over a dubious spot. Finally, he knows how to walk by himself, like a child

---
48 *Appui.*

Fels, trained and ridden by Lt. Colonel Gerhardt, Chief Rider at the School of Hanover, circa 1925. The positions of the two horses are nearly identical. And yet a world separates them. As René Bacharach noted in *L'Éperon* **of June 1965: Fels is compressed on himself"** (Steinbrecht). **Vallerine "is left as free as possible"** (Faverot).

from whom one has taken away his boundaries."

"The horse who has a habit of stiffening against the hand has a thousand chances of falling on his knees when the hand fails him. Supposing even that the hand would be still there, should he come to stumble, the violent action of the hand would propagate an immediate violent jerk through to the extremities pressing the ground and adding an immense weight whether to a limb that is flexing, or to the supporting limbs that are needed to come instinctively to the rescue of the one about to make a misstep."

Lightness also represents an irreplaceable advantage for the improvement of horses with defective constitutions. Knowing that

Vallerine, trained and ridden by Captain Beudant in 1925.

lightness of the jaw produces the relaxation of the whole horse, and knowing that horses of excellent constitution are rare, and consequently expensive, we believe that the relaxations (flexions) of the jaw done well are extremely useful in the dressage that we are studying.

General Decarpentry had the same way of seeing things. He wrote (*Équitation Academique*, 1949, p. 22), "Lightness manifests itself, outside of the perfection of movement, in the mobility of the jaw and by the flexibility of the haunches, so intimately connected by their reciprocal reactions that it is impossible to attribute to one of them the priority of decisive influence on the other."

Today the rider seeks to obtain from his horse the regularity of mechanized precision. Previously, this had not been a goal sought in training, and I think, for well-founded reasons.

One must not confuse the precise with the correct. Precision requires the geometric regularity of figures executed at a precise moment. Correctness requires, before anything else, that in the realization of the movements, the true attributes of equestrian art to be preserved.

Precision requires, for example, that the horse change lead or start a volte at a specific point. It is only a secondary consideration that attention is paid to the quality of the change of lead or the volte. Correct dressage, on the contrary, before being occupied with the exact place to execute figures, has a primary concern that the figures are executed with respect to sound forms of School horsemanship (*rassembler* and its requirements).

I believe that equestrian correction, which itself is obtained only in true lightness, is essential. I am in accord with the principle of the Italian riders, cited by Beudant (*Souvenirs Équestres*, (*Equestrian Memories*) 1934, p. 58): "Constrain the horse to do what you want, but once he does what you want, let him do it as he wants."

Then is there no usefulness in contact (*appui*)? Yes, there is. It can be useful in outdoor horsemanship, jumping, races, and also at the beginning of work for the horse destined for School horsemanship, so that he does not become confused between true lightness and the noisy chomping on the bit characteristic of the false lightness of a horse of whom one has demanded the relaxation of the jaw too soon, that is to say when his general flexibility cannot yet support it without risk.

In truth, lightness is a dangerous weapon for the rider that uses it poorly. That is why one could advise, before seeking the mobility of the jaw, to let the horse pass through a stage where the rider lets him take a certain contact (*appui*) while confirming him in a position from which the rider can, without danger, make the horse work in healthy lightness.

The important and difficult thing is to know at what moment one can, without fear, move on from contact to the relaxation of the jaw. In effect, even if the latter technique has inconveniences in the beginning, contact, when it is badly done, can prevent one from reaching a degree of confidant lightness.

There is no reason at all for contact to be used within the domain of academic dressage.[49]

---

49 Is there any other reason for it to be in the domain of elementary dressage or horsemanship for sport? One could, along with the military *écuyers* of the highest renown from the XVIII century, think not. This has been expressed, in the clearest manner, by M. Ducroc de Chabannes, former *écuyer* from the School at Saumur in his *Cours d'Équitation ou résumé des principes de M.*

Robersart II, trained and ridden by Captain Beudant in 1915. Trot with sustained extension. "At this gait, the horse appears not to touch the ground, and each foreleg always presents its greatest extension. To produce such a thrust, the upper leg muscles are extremely contracted and the hocks deploy with an activity that is amazing."

"The hallmark of *Haute École*, of scholarly horsemanship, artistic, higher dressage, or whatever one would call it, is not found in the more or less extraordinary movements, but in perfect lightness, whether the movements are simple or complicated."

"Lightness finds its witness, before anything else, in the submission of the jaw...."

"The mobility of the jaw not only demonstrates his submission. The flexibility of this region goes further, provoking the flexibility of the neck, then the flexibility of the other *ressorts* (joints), by way of the correlation existing instinctively among all muscular contractions." (L'Hotte, *Questions Équestres*, 1906, Chap. III)

---

d'Auvergne (1827) [Horsemanship Course or Summary of the Principles of Mr. D'Auvergne]). He said (p. 87) that the talent of a rider consists in maintaining the horse in balance and in being able to judge the balance if the horse has gaits that are cadenced, frank, and light, and the horse "does not seek any support on the hand." (N.F.T.)

THE HORSE "ON THE HAND"

AND THE HORSE "BEHIND THE HAND"

Each of the two manners has its partisans. The first (the horse on the hand) is the preference of those who find it a way to guide the horse more easily. Their horses execute the exercises with exactitude. But as we have said above, precision is not in itself correct, and it only has value if correctness is obtained. Never precision before correctness. The horse with innately beautiful conformation and gaits acquires a sleepy and unhappy attitude when one takes up a strong contact.

Contact with pressure or support presents no other interest than facilitating the guidance of the horse, which seems for the "modern *écuyer*" to be seen as a step above any other consideration.

In the old school horsemanship, the "ease of guidance" was meaningless if the horse was not *also* flexible, light, and brilliant.

What are the causes of the sleepy attitude of which we spoke? They are the contractions that are produced in the horse and the rider. In the rider, because he is preoccupied by the concern of making an aid intervene at a well determined moment; in the horse, because the lack of mobilization of the jaw corresponds to a constraint that is transmitted along the neck and the spinal column to all parts of his body.

One could say that the rider is always more or less contracted when he must present himself before a jury. This nervousness could be notably diminished if, as we have said above, the precision requirements would not be assessed by the judges until the characteristics of School horsemanship were satisfied. For example, when the horse must make fifteen changes of lead "*a tempi*," it should be secondary that they make thirteen or seventeen if these changes were impeccable from the academic point of view.

And why should the rider be penalized for having exceeded the prescribed time if he has otherwise proved that his mount satisfies the conditions of purely equestrian requirements? To impose a determined duration for a test nearly amounts to imposing a model of the horse, which all the contestants would have to seek to emulate so as not to take a supplementary risk of penalization.

Between any two horses, as similar as they may be, there is still a difference, not only in gaits, but in the individual cadence most suitable for each horse to give his best performance.

For example, one horse has a trot more *"écouté"* (more cadenced) than the other, but so as to not exceed the time allowed, the rider is forced to push the gait like the train driver who must meet the schedule, and the horse ends up losing the cadence that gave his trot its correctness and beauty.

Furthermore, to come back to the horse that is in front of the leg and on the hand, let us take note that such conditions bring him to find the *"concentration"* (collection) of the airs difficult. I believe that these conditions render obtaining a correct *rassembler* impossible. In the *rassembler*, the horse is balanced between the legs that create impulsion and the hand that receives it, which action can only be produced if the horse is light, because then the holding aids do not upset his balance. He can, from that balance, instead of pushing himself forward, direct his impulsion upward while cadencing his movements.

With regard to piaffe, Wachter wrote (*Aperçus Équestres*, 1862, p. 153), "this requires a horse with mobility of jaw and neck that leaves nothing to be desired so that the piaffe does not become a stamping, and it should not resemble, because of a clumsy pressure on the hand, one of those crooked scales in which a heavier tray always tends to overload in the same direction, and upsets the equilibrium that one seeks to establish between the two extremities of the balancing lever."

In *Ano Hipico Portugues* "The Portuguese Equestrian Year" (1956 – 1957) the French Colonel Challan-Belval defended a point of view similar to our own on the practice of the piaffe. Speaking of the contact of the mouth with the hand, he wrote:

"...When we wish to approach this perfection called the piaffe, this light contact is transformed of itself into a simple sentiment of the mouth obtained from only the weight of the reins, without any intervention of the hand. But this is possible only if at the contact of the legs; the horse bends the loins and croup and, with this flexibility, makes the hocks come under the body. The horse is in balance between the hand and legs. At this moment, the material tension on the reins is not entirely concrete, there is hardly any remaining; their moral tension must suffice. It is 'liberty on parole.' But if the hand intervenes, as little as it may to re-establish or maintain a material contact, the charm is ruptured, and with it, the perfect balance necessary to the piaffe."

Formoso, trained by Alfredo Conde, ridden by João Trigueiros de Aragão. Piaffe. "Grace on a horse." John Paget.

After this impeccable explanation, we can only rally ourselves to Baucher's concept that requires the horse to be "in front of the legs and behind the hand" – giving this expression its true meaning, and not the false interpretation of *acculement* (sucking back reporting too much weight on the back end while refusing to go forward); General L'Hotte fortunately added, "... as he grows in the withers at the same time that he flows in front of the legs." (*Un Officier de Cavalerie*, "A Cavalry Officer" 1905, p. 245)

Therefore, as it applies to a horse that is light and in front of the legs, there is nothing to let us say that the horse that does not take up contact (*appui*) with his bits is in *acculement*. And despite the fact that the realization of these conditions requires an uncommon tact, the school rider must still seek to make his horse's training tend toward this ideal.

I will cite again, in support of my thesis, this reflection from Beudant (*Souvenirs Équestres*, "Equestrian Memories" 1934, p. 53):

"If a rider obtains a soft flexible jaw with the reins semi-taut or even floating, he should not believe that his horse is in a void and that he has escaped the hand.

"It is not that at all: over an obstacle, at a lengthened trot, at the canter, in the passage, etc., the horse that is not light is, although well placed (in *ramener*), ordinarily 'outside of the hand.' On the contrary, the horse appearing 'in a void' is, even when not placed (in *ramener,*) in balance, if he is light, and is more in hand than if he pulls."

"All the same, the feel on the hand, the contact, is real, and when in the slightly open mouth, the tongue tastes the light touch of the bit, impressed only by the weight of the reins, whatever the position of the horse's head may be, this is harmony, the perfect accord of the forces of the rider and his horse."

After having read the words of this man, who was one of the greatest practitioners of the Baucher's last manner, how could one not be convinced? How could one not believe meanwhile, that to attain the extraordinary results that he obtained in the dressage of his horses, Beudant actually had recourse to the most complicated of Baucherist procedures? With an unbelievable modesty and an uncommon prudence, not considering himself a skilled enough rider to practice the simultaneous use of the aids, he applied, mounted, the principle *hand without legs, legs without hand* and in hand, he used the flexions, so as to prevent the bad results of the *effet d'ensemble* badly applied.

And it is again in the genial Beudant that the advocates of contact (*appui*) see themselves refuted. In the same *Souvenirs Équestres* "Equestrian Memories" (p. 62), he speaks of "the fixed hand on semi-taut reins," and described how, when he had become a semi-invalid, he used his hands on his mare Vallerine: "Only after having obtained the correct position with a fixed hand, would I need to let the reins loosen, to lower the hand and have Vallerine light and chomping her bit on a descent of the hand, not on a fixed point. (Important!)"

What is the principle of the flexion of the jaw? "The rider inflicts pressure on the horse until he yields, until he obeys. To cease to give him discomfort is to say to the horse, "You have done what I have ordered!" (Raabe, *Méthode de Haute École d'Équitation*, "Method of High School Horsemanship"1863, p. 126.) We find here again, the principle of the freedom from the action afforded the horse as soon as he understands the order that the rider has given him. The rider imposes his will on the horse, provoking discomfort until the horse yields. If the rider maintains the pressure permanently, he maintains a discomfort that his mount can only deliver himself from by hardening himself against it. This hardening is transmitted throughout the horse, "because the resistances sustain each other." (L'Hotte, *Questions Équestres*, "Equestrian Questions" 1906, p. 36.) One could conclude that "equitation on the hand" carries in itself the peril of deadening the horse by taking away the natural brilliance that can exist only in a light horse.

We have shown that without complete lightness, the correct execution of certain airs, such as piaffe, passage, transitions from one to the other and vice versa, is absolutely impossible. General Decarpentry specifies (*Piaffer et Passage*, 1932) that the use of the *hand without the leg, and the leg without the hand*, is the only means of arriving at a level of perfection in the transitions into and out of these airs. It is normal to be so, because we know that the engagement of the hindquarters corresponds to a lightening of the mouth. In the airs, like piaffe and passage requiring a high degree of *rassembler*, it is therefore an ill-fated misinterpretation to support the horse with a physical contact. If he is well balanced and consequently light, this supporting contact will prevent him from being able to make these airs correct and imposing, as they should be when they are executed in *rassembler*.

General Decarpentry, aptly wrote of what would become of Baucherism, making allusion to the insufficiency of *rassembler* and *mise en main* in many horses (*Baucher et son École*, 1948, p. 139(*Baucher and his School*, Xenophon Press 2011), "The lightness of these (incorrect) horses is anything other than a reduction in their contact coming at the same time from the shortening of the front end and the limitation of the efforts of the hindquarters, without a useful *rassembler*."

The question becomes clear and could theoretically be summarized as follows: the balanced horse lightens himself. Since the goal of dressage is to balance the horse, lightness inevitably becomes a sign of balance. If the rider obtains balance, he must give the greatest possible liberty to his horse, so that the horse can maintain it himself. A force like a supporting contact (*appui*), useless in the management of balance, is not only unfavorable to that balance if it is maintained for a long time, it also leads to a loss of balance.

In conclusion, contact is not a suitable means to be used by those who want to balance their horses for the purpose of practicing true School horsemanship. What a pity that this question, so easy to explain theoretically – and that has come to be considered as the touchstone of true dressage – is so difficult to put into practice!

HOLDING THE REINS

Another point meriting attention is the one concerning the way the reins are held. The FEI regulation (1958, Par. 416) prescribes riding with separated reins. This rule has been modified and today (1971), the rider can hold all four reins in the left hand, with the right hand posed on the two right reins.

We know that there are horses that can be managed better with the reins in one hand, others with the reins separated; and also that there are riders who are more skilled while using their reins in one manner or the other. We do not see the necessity to standardize the way to hold the reins, to create a "standard" rider for whom one or the other way of holding the reins adds or withdraws merit.

There are cases where a practical reason can lead to a preference to ride with the reins in one hand. General Faverot de Kerbrech (*Dressage Méthodique du Cheval de Selle....* 1891, p.158, *Methodical Dressage of the Riding Horse*, Xenophon Press 2010) said about the repeated changes of lead, "Take his reins in one hand," and Beudant (*Souvenirs Équestres*, 1934, p. 53): "It is from observation and not from a scientific theory that we learn that the two hands used together never have the fixity, nor do they have the appropriate soft mobility of the single hand." To clarify his remark, he gives an example that we have all noticed at one time or another. If we carry a glassful of water in one hand, it does not spill; but if we carry it in two hands, it almost always spills. So, to seek the fixity of the horse's head, it is evidently an error to ride with separated reins. The possibility of riding with the reins in one hand, now allowed by the regulations, ought to be seriously considered by contestants.

JUDGING CRITERIA

General Decarpentry thought it a good thing that there was a Germanic manner and a French manner each with its own characteristics. But what appears to me a fault is that the juries, because of the training of the judges, give advantage to German criteria. Also, I wish that France, heir to a style that should stand for the glory of riding, would organize tests of School horsemanship whose programs could be those of the FEI but of which the judging criteria would be positively equestrian.

In truth, if School horsemanship is "the poetry of equitation" (Baucher); if it is an art that is related to "the art of choreography, to classical ballet" (Decarpentry); if it is "transcendental horsemanship" (Baucher); if "the dressage of the horse is the best complement to the education of man" (Gustave le Bon); if "High School separates those who are only capable of practicing an instinctive horsemanship from those who can practice a rational horsemanship...," and if "this separation is similar to the line of demarcation that exists between the vulgar and the beautiful, the prose of the rest of the world from that of Buffon[50], the fiddler and Paganini[51]" (Raabe); if "when I feel my horse bend at my every wish, and responding without any resistance to my thoughts, execute with grace and a perfect lightness every movement that I ask of him, I am so happy that, far from my feeling suffering from the clamors of envy and ingratitude of the plagiarists, I have only one desire, to make them share my happiness" (Baucher); if it is true that School horsemanship is all that, how can it accommodate supporting contact,however little pronounced it may be?

If the horse is not considered a being that must be unconditionally submissive as the German School understands it, but as a friend that collaborates in a communal equestrian work of art, the

---

50 Georges-Louis Leclerc, Comte de Buffon (7 September 1707-16 April 1788) was a French naturalist, mathematician, cosmologist, and encyclopedic author that was a precursor of Darwin.
51 Niccolò Paganini, (1782-1840) celebrated Italian violin virtuoso and composer.

dramatic desire expressed by General L'Hotte that his last three horses – Glorieux, Domfront, and Insensé – be put down after his death makes sense. Without a doubt and with some disdain, he feared that if they were not put down, they would have been mistreated, those horses he had considered as a part of himself.

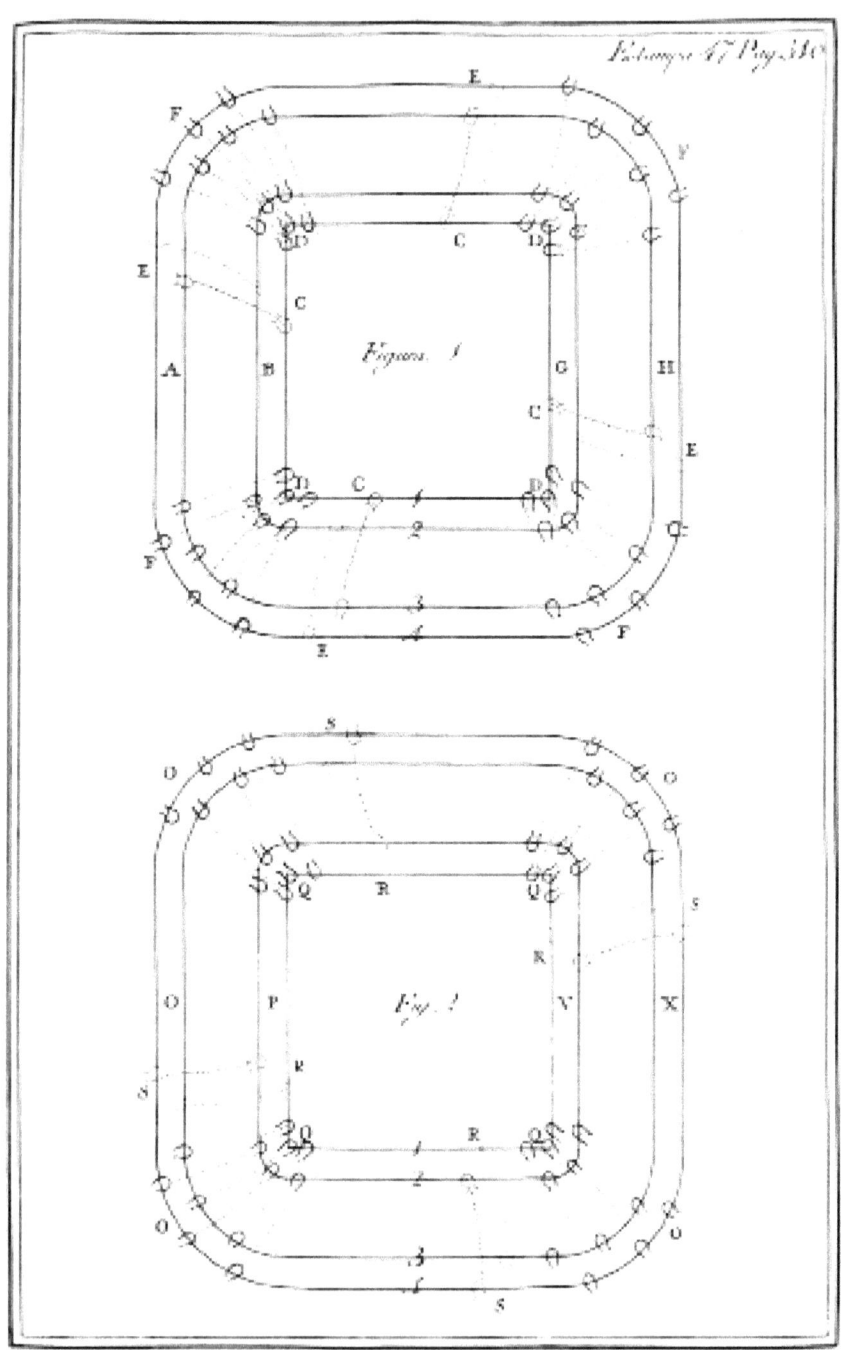

Reversed square voltes to the right and to the left.

CHAPTER 2

CONTEMPORARY ACADEMIC HORSEMANSHIP

IN PORTUGAL

Within the panorama of international academic dressage, let us examine what is happening today in Portugal, a country that possesses a tradition in the art that occupies us now.

We have already analyzed the equestrian merit of the Marquis de Marialva and the influence of the work of Manoel Carlos de Andrade all the way up to our times.

Since this monumental work, outside of a translation of *Méthode d'Équitation* (Method of Equitation) by Baucher, in Portugal there have not been any important books published, nor translations of works on academic dressage, the teaching of which would have been valuable. Many books are unavailable to Portuguese *écuyers*, although they have always been interested in French dressage and practiced it. They have found only elements of it in a few articles and in compilations of works. So what they have been inspired with is better known by oral tradition and hearsay than by the reading and meditation so necessary to the resolution of difficult problems in the horsemanship of *Haute École*.

School horsemanship is practiced in Portugal by some cavalry officers, some civilian *écuyers*, and by Tauromachic (bullfighting) riders. I say officers because I cannot unfortunately speak of military schools, as proper academic dressage is only taught in a very rudimentary fashion, as much quantitatively as qualitatively.

In fact the Portuguese, military or civilians, who maintain a love of the "Noble Art" and dedicate themselves to the highest expression of equestrian activity, are the exceptions to the rule.

The methods employed by the officers' aim at the preparation of their horses for the FEI tests. Within the limit of the rules to which they must hold, they have a tendency to conform to the concepts of the French School. If we see them adopt certain techniques from the

German School, it is because they recognize the propensity of the juries to establish their rankings according to Germanic criteria. Can we blame them, since they are representatives of their country in international competitions?

The practice of academic dressage by civilians is limited to a few enthusiasts who have neither *manèges* in which to practice nor teachers for their training, with the exception of the school of my dear master and friend, Nuno Oliveira, passionate practitioner and teacher of *Haute École*, who succeeded in instilling in his students a taste for academic dressage. That is where we are now.

BULLFIGHTING HORSEMANSHIP

AND ITS MERIT IN RELATION TO DRESSAGE

By national taste, we like to have very handy horses, even if it is only to ride in the country. Furthermore, Iberian peninsula horses allow us to practice quite easily a collected horsemanship that is used in cutting cattle, in the rapid coming and going of hare coursing, and finally in bullfighting from horseback.

In Tauromachic horsemanship, do we practice school horsemanship?

Even if Tauromachic horsemanship is not academic dressage, it is, I believe, the only equestrian activity proving that the horses it uses are truly "finished" as School horses.

The submission, the balance, the brilliance, and the mobility that result from dressage are very strenuously put to the test because the bull is not joking. A very small part of the public is alert enough to be able to take into account the extraordinary quality of the work of the horse and his rider.

If a horse that was perfectly trained academically could not be used for bullfighting, it still would have a good reason. Even so, I want to point out that the execution of movements that the horse would have to make in the arena, even before he would get in front of the bull, would be proof enough of the quality of his training.

We should add, for the case that occupies us now: ...is the horse willing and submissive enough to gallop toward the bull from whom the rider will provoke a charge, and allow the rider to stick the bull with a banderilla (an ornamented dart with barbs used by banderilleros for sticking into the neck or shoulder of the bull), each pass closer than the last, often with the stirrup between the horns, only to escape the bull with precision, letting him charge into a void.

How should a good bullfighting horse be defined? By the qualities that have always been asked of him, and have not varied to this day.

According to the *Reglas de Torear* "Rules of Bullfighting" by the Count of Bornos (1644): "The bullfighting horse must be more than six years old, to have enough size (we will see later on what this means), to be easy to ride, to have a "good mouth" and a good loin, to have solid and agile legs, to be capable of "departing from the movement of the hand" without the aid of the spurs....

"He must be docile, noble, courageous, obedient to the exercises that are suitable to the bullfighting arena, like sudden starts and stops, ultra-rapid runs over the necessary distances, the halts on the haunches, from very collected canter, similar to a *parade*, without sticking the forelegs into the ground, without taking the reins from the hand, shaking the head, diving behind the bit or thrusting above it, with the halts executed very straight and the horse controlled behind and in front."

The following reference is borrowed from the work by my friend Fernando de Sommer d'Andrade, *Toureio a Cavalo,* "Bullfighting from Horseback," published in Lisbon in 1966. This book has not yet been translated, and I am pleased to present, in its earliest quote in English, this commentary that F. d'Andrade has made. In all of the pages that follow where there is a question of Tauromachic horsemanship, there are substantial extracts of his text that he has authorized me to reproduce. They explain, better than I could have done, the merits of Tauromachic horsemanship compared to School dressage.

Fernando d'Andrade, analyzing the passage, cited above from the Count de Bornos, tells us:

"***A depart on the hand without the aid of the spur*** indicates that the horse must not be behind the hand, but rather have just the right contact and be ready to leap forward, on the simple loosening of the fingers, exactly like a horse that we would consider today to be perfectly trained.

"*To provide for ultra-rapid runs over the necessary distances*, the perfectly submissive horse must stop very rapidly, but without shock or jerky movements denoting, in general, bad training.

"*Dominated behind and in front* means that the horse mobilizes his shoulders as easily as his haunches on the indications of the aids, which is necessary to perform the halts without traversing himself, the same as he would to execute lateral movements well."

These requirements of the Count de Bornos hardly have to be modified to describe a good modern bullfighting horse. (I continue here,

DVM José Varela Cid.
A scramble to the extreme limit of a fall, but nobody falls down. Find the bull: the left horn with its leather cap, obligatory in Portugal, is visible behind the horse.

and in the pages that follow, to cite F. d'Andrade.)

The horses used before were small in size. Those that were taller than 1.50 m. (14.3HH) were considered large. Crossing and improvements in breeding have allowed larger horses than in other times. The size preferred today is between 1.54 m. and 1.58 m. (15-15.2HH.) Smaller animals have less force, and weighing less, eventually they are more likely to be affected by an eventual collision with the bull. On the smaller horse the rider is lower to the ground and if he is tall, may even appear a little ridiculous. Horses taller than 1.60 m. (15.3HH) are too large. They are considered less skilled. Their longer stride makes their maneuvering more difficult in the small Portuguese arena.

Nevertheless these rules have their exceptions, and we can also say that among the horses, small or large, some are good, strong, and willing, and others are bad, weak and *ramingues* (those who will not move off the spur.)

The most appropriate breed, in the past, was the Jennet from Spain. Horses of other origin were too heavy and too slow or did not have good enough mouths, or good enough character. Today, when crosses with blood horses are in vogue, we can say without any doubt, that the best are the Iberian peninsular horses that have strength, even though this characteristic might be difficult to find in them. Blood horses with great scope, selected by tests of speed at the end of the last century and at the beginning of this one, lack strength in the slow gaits, a serious obstacle to obtaining the training necessary for facing a bull with precision at a deliberate pace. The lack of strength of the horse forces the bullfighter into using speed to exploit opportunities instead of calmly provoking the attacks of the bull while remaining master of the situation.

The crossbreeds can be used on condition that their temperament, their morale, their character allow the quality of dressage defined by Count de Bornos. But such a quality is found somewhat rarely in a cross of a peninsular horse with an Arab or Thoroughbred because even though frequently they have good loins, strength, and impulsion, they are just as frequently found to be nervous, irritable, malicious, indocile, coward, with difficult mouths and little disposition to engage the hindquarters.

A good Spanish horse with sufficient strength and whose character and conformation belong to the breed that has been selected over the centuries for a similar type of use in warfare for single combat, may be brought, with ordinary training administered by an average

D.V.M. José Varela Cid
At the moment when the banderille is planted, the bull strikes a void.

instinctive rider, to be a horse suitable for bullfighting. But with a horse presenting the difficulties coming from blood, it requires a School rider with an equestrian quality sufficient to be able to resolve the training problems that arise. Even more so, if the rider has an ambition for the highest Tauromachic results. If he does not have this ambition, the search for a blood horse for bullfighting is not justified.

The horse is a loyal servant that puts his body and his personality at our disposal to help us. He helps us with an attention approaching perfection when he is brought along to perceive our intentions, thanks to honest and delicate methods of persuasion. If he is trained with brutality, he can become a slave and therefore be completely submissive. However, trained thusly, he loses his personality and his desire to come to the aid of his rider, not bringing the rider good will and even the initiative that so often saves a difficult situation which the rider would not be able to escape by himself.

The fear that the rider inspires in the horse is not always superior to that which a danger provokes. So it is at the very moment when his obedience would be the most necessary that he will be least willing to obey and the horse will force his rider to change his plan of attack on the bull. Persuasion allows us to make the horse a servant who also becomes our friend. Roughness only results in making an apathetic or undisciplined slave.

So as to never use roughness when wanting to make a horse understand what is expected of him, one must know how to proceed, what method to follow to gradually instill in him the significance of the aids. At the same time, one must make him practice the appropriate and progressive gymnastics that make it possible for him to satisfy the requirements of the rider.

The good bullfighting rider must attain quite a high equestrian quality. His body must appear tranquil. His aids must be discrete and even invisible. In particular, the bridle hand must seem to be completely immobile. The legs must fall naturally and seem to be softly touching the horse. It is a fault to push them to the rear or to carry them forward and worse yet, to swing back and forth, or against the flank, even in relation to the movements of the horse, If allowed to swing unnecessarily their actions cannot be delicate, nor accurate and measured, but are, on the contrary, sudden and abrupt.

The equestrian qualities of the rider are evidenced by the behavior of the horse. A horse well-trained, ridden by a good rider, obeys at the slightest indication, without nervousness and without hesitation. A horse whose neck is stiff, the jaw clenched, who either pulls or puts himself behind the hand or who gets mad, proves that the training is defective or that he is ridden by a bad rider. It appears in every way that the horse-rider partnership is not good. One hardly needs to state that it is the quality of this partnership that is the principal requirement for Portuguese bullfighting.

Right after that, one must immediately cite the "courage" of the rider. It expresses itself in different ways.

One type of bravery is of a nervous character, impulsive and reacts to danger with a brusque push. The need to act becomes subconscious and without thinking, the rider, come what may, clenches his teeth, tenses his muscles, and without controlling himself, controlling his horse even less, he attacks....It's the type of valor that incites the rider to rush forward.

This is spectacular, without a doubt, because this kind of action, unplanned, surprises the public who cannot figure out what is happening. His nervous tension provokes a profound "Oh!" of disappointment in case of failure or ovations in case of success.

In the course of a bullfighting tournament, the rider often has recourse to this form of valor, or in default, it is the horse himself that, because of his imperfect dressage or because of a lack of decisiveness of the rider, goes all alone to brush up against the danger, at full speed, without letting himself be controlled.

The other form of valor, the true courage, is that which allows one to face danger with enough serenity to be able to think rationally and control oneself.

When the horse is perfectly *dressé* (trained) and has the natural qualities necessary to be able to get out of a difficult "pass" without too much effort, he confronts the danger with calm and self-assurance and accepts orders at every moment of the "attacks."

If the rider possesses true courage and perfectly controls his nerves in every moment of danger, he is then able to execute the "pass" with perfect smoothness, each phase being well marked because his aids have been gentle, graduated, of the right intensity, smooth and without hesitation.

The rider and the horse have that much more time to assess the danger than when the attack has been conducted more slowly. The difficulty lies in keeping the necessary calm. The rider succeeds in directing the fight slowly if he is more courageous and also if his horse is better trained, he can lead him more slowly. An additional advantage of a slow pace is that it leaves the public not only the time but also the calm necessary to appreciate the details of each "pass."

A Tauromachic rider who fights with impetuosity has much less merit than one who fights slowly because one that goes quickly might have a much less trained horse, have less courage, or execute "passes" much less well. Even if speed is not caused by any of these faults, it can mask them, not leaving time for the spectator to analyze what is going on. It provokes in the rider a nervous tension which affects the quality of his judgment....

I think it is useful to complete this very detailed analysis by F. Andrade with what he also said about "Handling a horse in the Arena," where his competence, as I see it, enlightens us better than any other critique of the equestrian art of bullfighting has ever done. So I will

**Temporal, trained and ridden by João Nuncio.
Despite the danger, even at "the moment of truth," the horse is light.**

continue to quote him:

"... We have said that the horse must be very well trained, and we have indicated the evaluation that we have made of the equestrian quality

Xelim, trained and by João Nuncio and ridden by José Nuncio, his son, playfully avoids the bull's charge, whose sharp horns have been left uncovered. (As is the rule in Spain but not in Portugal).

of the rider and that of the dressage of his horse, but we have not yet said which exercises should be practiced.

A good bullfighting horse must be perfectly finished in the School work.

Perfectly relaxed and collected, he must be able to adopt any balance demanded of him, depart forward or to the rear without effort, to go on two tracks in shoulder-in or haunches-in at the walk, trot, or canter on the straight or on curves as well on the left hand as on the right. He must be able to instantly change the gait, speed, or direction, without effort or jerkiness, with all the adjustments that the rider demands. Often, the horses that we see fighting bulls make a quick volte, very tight, depart abruptly at the extended canter or stop short, but too frequently, they do not correctly make a larger and slower circle or a variation in a gait that is progressive and at a desirable rate!

They should know how to piaffe, passage, canter in terre-à-terre (movement in which the horse rocks from back end to forehand in an elevated movement that shows much collection and gains little ground with each stride), do a courbette[52], a pirouette, etc., not only for the courtesies[53], but also in the course of the preparation for a "pass," because they must entertain the public with School airs, in the intervals that separate the attacks with the *banderillas*.

What must be perfected to the maximum in the bullfighting horse is his work at the canter because it is at this gait that they practice the "passes" and fight the bull. The most important points are: departs on the correct lead, ability to slow down smoothly, the stops, changes of lead on the straight and the circle, canter sideways from one side to the other – on the lead on the side to which the horse is coming out sideways (half-pass) or on the opposite lead (shoulder-in).

This last work, little used, is an essential exercise for the perfect execution of the head-on attack, without letting the horse lead with his

---

52 These are classic courbettes. The best definition that I have found is that in the *Dictionnaire by Guillet* (1678): "The courbettes are jumps of medium height that the horse makes by first raising both his forefeet in the air, and then both hind feet follow in an equal cadence: in a way that the hind legs come under together after the forefeet have touched the ground, in continuous, regular repetitions." (NFT)
53 Spectacular presentations of the horses and salutes from the riders before the fight. (NFT)

haunches uncontrollably. The majority of bullfighting riders confuse a horse that is nervously balanced on the hindquarters with a horse in *rassembler*. Having a horse excited and very much on the hindquarters does not mean that he is in *rassembler* with impulsion. Most of the time the exaggerated balance on the haunches creates too much delay and requires an excessive effort on the part of horse to depart and get off to a good start. Furthermore, the surcharge of weight on the haunches makes the mobilization of the croup difficult and obliges riders to use the spur constantly, one of the factors that unnerves the horses. They are led, in the end, to *aculement* (when the horse is back on his heels and refuses to go forward diligently) from the practice of extremely violent stops, constant mobilization of the forehand, and much less pronounced mobilization of the hindquarters in the movements on two tracks. Since these exercises are obtained by a rein of opposition with an excessive lateral displacement of the horse, they accentuate the *aculement* by opposing the movement forward.

The *aculement* and excitement, provoking heightened movements of the forelegs and the excessive mobility of the jaw, certainly give brilliance to the preparation for the "pass" that we are used to seeing. However, at the moment of moving off, the horse has a tendency to get out of hand, the rider loses gentleness in the control of the horse, seeing himself obliged to resort to an abrupt half-halt that provokes *aculement* again when he wants to retake command. But at the moment of truth, so that the "meeting[54]" happens entirely within the rules, the horse must not pass in a straight line in front of the bull, nor bend only to extricate his forehand or, at least, to accentuate the escape of the forehand more than the hindquarters by traversing himself. He must, on the contrary, move his whole body laterally, maintaining himself parallel to his initial trajectory or even moving his hindquarters away slightly more than his forehand. It is only after passing the bull's head that the horse should bend himself away from the right horn, making a fragment of a reversed pirouette[55] from right to left in the right shoulder-in to enter the bull's "terrain."[56]

The horse must canter on the right lead even as he moves his body to the left, which is obtained by an intermediate action of the right rein that allows for the horse, at the same time, to turn his head slightly to the right, so he can look at the bull. The horse is then in horizontal

---

54 The moment when the horse gets closest to the bull. (NFT)
55 Turn on the forehand
56 That is to say to pass the bull's head in the direction of the animal's tail(NFT)

Kasavubu, trained and ridden by José-Luis de Sommer d'Andrade. Face to face: the bull is going to get hit while the horse avoids him by remaining calm and supple.

balance, meaning his weight is equally divided on the forehand and the hindquarters, but the hind legs are engaged well under his body and he is always ready to temporarily modify his balance, by surcharging either the shoulders or the haunches, according to the necessity of the moment. He must canter with great impulsion, well collected, but calm and relaxed..."

One can understand that in a frontal attack – the true one, as Fernando d'Andrade just described to us – the difficulty of planting the *banderilla* when the bull's head is "at the stirrup" in fact increases because the two trajectories are almost directly opposed, their speeds are added to each other and the rider must remain calm.

The preparation for the "pass," having the eye for the distance, mastering the precision of execution, possessing the "heart" that is necessary to perfect each attack, achieving the instantaneous execution that the rider demands of his horse, requires a great finesse in dressage and extraordinary equestrian qualities.

Another quality that must be added to the solid technical knowledge of bullfighting, is a "feeling" for the bull's behavior and mood that allows the rider to make him move, to handle him from afar according to the rider's will, to "dominate" him. There is also required of this rider, a genuine artistic sense that allows him to maintain his discretion, elegance, and brilliance in this distinctively Portuguese Tauromachic fencing match that does not have a tragic end.[57]

All this seems quite complicated to someone who has never seen bullfighting on horseback, but those who have attended a good Portuguese Tauromachic tournament will understand that the art of combat on horseback has been the basis of equestrian art, that is to say, academic dressage. It is said that horsemanship must evolve, adapt, etc. But when I see what has not evolved, what a difference! That is what I prefer.

THE HORSE FAIR AT GOLEGÃ

There are trading places for bullfighting horses, the principal market of which is held at the annual fair at Golegã (on Saint Martin's Day, 11 November). One can see there a style of horsemanship that could be called Golegan or Ribatejan, that is to say, from the valley of the River Tejo. The riders who come to present their horses in Golegã

---

[57] There is no putting to death in a Portuguese bullfight. The bull's horns are sheathed in leather caps that resemble dice cups so that the risks of penetrating wounds, if not painful contusions, are eliminated. This protection allows for the rider, after he has planted a certain number of *banderillas*, to be replaced in the arena by a group of young men on foot. One of these young men makes the bull charge him, seizes his head between the horns, gripping him there, and the others glom onto him to brake the bull's run until he stops. This is the *"pega"*, the catch. (N.F.T.)

**Trianero, trained and ridden by Alvaro Domeq.
Astonishing courage and virtuosity.**

want to sell them. And they ride trying to make them as brilliant as possible, in a fashion designed to dazzle the spectators. The facility with which the peninsular horses engage their hindquarters, the demonstrative and bragging behavior of our southern temperament, the extraordinary natural skill of the riders that often falls just short of virtuosity, all of this conspire to turn this fair into a spectacle that – even though it has aspects that could be criticized- is nevertheless the spontaneous product of the raw qualities of country life, without a doubt, but they are absolutely admirable from an equestrian point of view.

It is something hardly ordinary, and maybe even unique, that this provincial gathering of several dozen riders that present their horses, making them passage, piaffe, pirouette at the canter, etc., put into practice this thought of Commandant de Salins, "The great ambition of a rider must be to make his horse shine."

The ambiance of equestrian demonstrations in France, Italy, England, and Germany are not familiar to me. I do not believe one often encounters in those countries, as one does here in the villages near the Tejo, riders that make their horses prance with pride in the streets, or make them pirouette at top speed if they perceive that a young woman admires them from her window, or half-pass to the right or to the left, then on a rein-back, take off at a full-speed gallop attracting perhaps as well the attention of an eventual buyer. A scene of this genre can take place at any time of the year in the Ribatejan countryside, but most particularly during the fair in Golegã where all the riders of reputation in Portugal can be seen at the same time.

Outside of the acquisitions that one can make there, the attraction of this fair is the presentation of trained horses that are not for sale. One can admire the comings and goings of riders that take pleasure in exhibiting their mounts. It is almost all that remains to us of the equestrian carrousels of yesteryear.

What is the Ribatejan rider's ideal in horsemanship? He aspires to make his horse capable of executing the exercises that he would have to do if he needed to run a bull. So right away he has chosen the model that is the most favorable. Many connoisseurs consider the horsemanship of Golegã a deplorable spectacle and want to banish all that is practiced there, advising that riders take up a simple horsemanship with the sole preoccupation to exploit the natural gaits in a horizontal balance.

I too find that the *Haute École* that one sees in the Ribatejo has plenty of faults. However, I am not in agreement with the remedy indicated above. One must in effect recognize that we assist there at the manifestation of a skill outside of the ordinary, of a very Portuguese taste to shine, of an art of riding that has survived in our country, and that makes the horse the jewel and the legitimate pride of the rider.

The ability to practice the difficult movements on two tracks and on the straight with ease, even tainted with flaws, proves that the riders who show off have the skill to teach these movements to their horses. If this skill is a sign of equestrian tact, as I believe it is, they only need to discipline it. In horsemanship, tact is not taught, it can be developed and refined. To want to remedy to the faults of the Golegan horsemanship by making it obey the rules of riders whose goal is precision rather than brilliance, would stifle its artistic sense, which is its best quality.

The Ribatejan riders, whose horses work sitting too much on the hindquarters in passage or in the pirouettes, ameliorate these airs by making the horses alternate them with lengthening at the trot and at the canter.

We owe it to ourselves to maintain a skill that has become a part of our Portuguese equestrian patrimony, and that comes to us from bullfighting on horseback. Can we imagine one of our Tauromachic riders, traditionally dressed in the costume of the Louis XV era, riding a horse that goes with his nose on the ground?

"Extended" horsemanship presents plenty of interest and I am not opposed to it, as one might believe reading what I have to say. But Golegã is certainly not made for that style if one admits that each type of horsemanship must thrive in its appropriate context. School horsemanship unfolds on an elevated level, and when I meet followers of sport horsemanship who are not disposed to recognize that, I am reminded of the opinion of a friend of mine who declared, "I prefer the grape to the wine."

Peninsular horses are worked by the majority of riders from the Ribatejo, in the collected gaits that they find favorable to the horses' training. Some people are of the opinion that precisely because these horses have gaits that are not very ample by nature, they must be worked to extend those gaits. I do not share this opinion because what must guide the trainer in working the horse are the conformation, temperament, and gaits, from which result what we call his natural balance. Our peninsular horses' constitution makes them put themselves into collected gaits with relative facility. I think that this aptitude should be emphasized in practicing a rational dressage. One can in fact observe that it is only after having worked our peninsular horses at collected gaits that we can make them take up extended gaits without too much difficulty.

What are the principal elements of their constitution that explain the difficulty in obtaining lengthenings? They are relatively weak hindquarters compared to an imposing front end, with a large head, thick neck, strong jaws that require local work of the forehand so that its position avoids the shifting of too much weight onto the haunches.

Besides, experience proves to us that there is not a lengthened canter more disagreeable than that of a peninsular horse that has not been balanced by his training from the beginning. In support of this assertion, we find in *L'Équitation raisonnée* (Ire éd., 1943, p. 72) by Commandant Licart, this quotation from Lenoble du Teil: "If the jaw and neck do not yield, the feeling of the hand is communicated to the hindquarters through a stiffened spinal column: the impulsion is thwarted." And Commandant Licart specifies (p. 49) that on the contrary, if the *ramener* is obtained, "the loin and the hocks of the horse, sheltered from the actions of the rider's hand, allow an increase in the engagement of the hind legs, the 'concentration of forces,' and the elevated movement of the legs."

All these remarks are justification for Golegan horsemanship that puts its horses on the haunches, and I think that it is good since it is in *this* position that the handling of peninsular horses is at its best. Since they are the breed of horse that was used by the Old School, one could even think that their dressage should culminate in successful School jumps. That it is not so is because Tauromachic horsemanship absorbs all the attention of the Golegan rider, who trains his horse either for his own personal satisfaction, or to improve the horse's value in the eyes of an eventual buyer, who will often be a bullfighting rider.

An example that best illustrates this it is the horse that tells the rider the exercises that correspond best to his temperament is the modern form of the School walk. This is an air that blood horses give us voluntarily and one understands that it does not present great difficulty in horses with ample gaits. Beudant defined the school walk (*Dressage du Cheval de Selle*, 1948, p. 58) as "a diminutive of the Spanish walk, a march at attention, pompous, solemn."

One can see well therefore the difference between the peninsular horse who, by his facility with putting himself on the haunches, has led to the practice of collected airs, and the blood horse that encourages the practice of the other airs like repeated flying changes of lead and the modern school walk of which we have spoken above.

HORSEMANSHIP METHODS

FROM THE VALLEY OF THE TEJO

The equestrian means that Golegan horsemanship uses derive principally from the Old School and early Baucherism. From the Old School remains a seated position of the horse, the use of a quite severe curb bit without the addition of a bridoon, and the use of a saddle *"à piquer"* (An XVIII century war saddle, see Commandant Licart, *Évolutions Équestres, à travers les ages*, Olivier Perrin Éditeur, Paris, 1963, p. 9.)

The horse moves on the haunches, head high, but he has not (as far as I know) been put to the pillars with the side reins and cavesson that the Old Masters used to push the horse into *ramener*. The constant preoccupation of riders who start training at the trot is to go straight away to the *rassembler*. They are attacking it too quickly, but with the justification that the more the horse is collected, the more he is balanced, and, by consequence, handy.

So, their error is not in the idea that the *rassembler* is essential to dressage, but in their false concept of the *rassembler*. It is because of that concept that they begin to bring together the extremities of the horse, as Baucher did in his First Manner, to draw from it a passage, and not with the idea of ameliorating the general equilibrium of the horse by gymnasticising his back.

However, plenty of horses do not cadence themselves immediately, so their riders, in too much of a hurry, begin to make them elevate the forelegs, and to associate them with the hind legs by a diagonal reflex; the passage is born of the succession of diagonal steps thus obtained. Then it takes one of the two following forms: either the horse lifts the forelegs a great deal but hardly advances because the hindquarters are squashed, or he throws the forelegs forward, offering too open a passage. Either one of these postures demonstrates a defective *rassembler* and an excessive haste in seeking the passage.

For me, the action of making the forearm rise by means of the stick is not reprehensible if it is used with horses who are "daisy cutters." If the hind legs are engaged and flexed as they ought to be, one obtains thereby much more brilliance and, in the case of a very nervous horse that jogs in place without advancing himself, or of horses that lack temperament, the raising of the forearms is the only way to get a passage.

In the same as one acts on the hindquarters with the stick, when working in hand, I see no reason that one cannot do the same on the forehand to lift and round the movement of the forelegs, so that the impulsion and the *rassembler* are not compromised. It is appropriate to complete the piaffe and passage by developing the aptitude of the horse to go from these airs to an impulsive and extended trot, and to come back to passage and piaffe, which is seen only exceptionally at Golegã, and is all to the honor of the riders that perform these transitions.

THE AIRS PRACTICED IN THE HORSEMANSHIP FROM THE VALLEY OF THE TEJO

As we have already let it be understood, the true (correct) work at the walk is not part of this horsemanship. The walk is often hurried, even lateral. The natural walk in equal four beats is hardly ever observed. Since the riders are looking for brilliance and a certain effect, they are not attached to correcting the gait, and we see them promenade in "*trottiner* (a hurried jog)!"

There is a variety of walk that some practice. It is the Spanish walk, sometimes called suspended walk, considered by the majority of equestrian authors as an artificial gait or a fancy gait. I am personally aligned with the opinion of Doctor Gustav Le Bon that "all the horse's natural gaits at liberty become artificial under the weight of a rider." I conclude that the Spanish walk is artificial at the same level as the rein-back or the work on two tracks. I do not see why they qualify the Spanish walk as artificial, all the while finding natural a series of lead changes "*a tempi*," or a transition from passage to piaffe, especially since, among the peninsular horses there are many that have an in-bred propensity to the *jambette*[58].

I think that the Spanish walk well-practiced is a very beneficial gymnastic. The normal walk being considered by Baucher to be the basis for dressage, the Spanish walk, which is none other than a walk in which the gestures are brought to the maximum of slow amplitude, has then all the benefits of collected walk and even the added advantage of developing the amplitude of gesture and the relaxation of the jaw.

The work at the trot, or work from the trot, is practiced on voltes,

---

58 (the extension of a single foreleg).

in the development of work on two tracks, in the passage, and in the piaffe. In their *appuyers* (half-passes), the Ribatejanos often commit the error of letting the haunches pass the shoulders. And we have already spoken enough of the defects in their passage and piaffe to conclude that in seeking them, they focus more to brilliance than on correctness.

The work at the canter is comprised of voltes, rapid pirouettes, changes of lead on the straight or in sudden changes of direction, halts from the gallop, immediately followed by rein-back, and departs at the gallop from the rein-back. This work, often executed with great dexterity shows the submission and the agility of the horse in movements that he will have to make in front of the bull. It is regrettable that the rider does not train his mount to pass from this work that excites him to other versions done in complete calm.

It is interesting to note that Captain Raabe referred to movements of this type in speaking of the *passade*. "The rider who, on a straight line, passes from the extended canter to the collected canter and who by half-pirouettes covers the same line several times, executes the *passade*. He may even make a change of lead at the end of each half-pirouette which allows him to execute this work along the wall. This exercise, well executed, denotes a true talent and a horse perfectly finished." (*Méthode de Haute École d'Équitation*, "Method of High School Horsemanship" 1863.)

It is too bad that this praise concerning the *passade* cannot entirely apply to the Ribatejan riders that practice it. And this is so, only because, after such brilliant movements, the horses cannot calm down. They demonstrate also that their horsemanship is the result of their own inspiration, and it leads them to a daily search for brilliant airs and not to the practice of exercises that gymnasticize, that calm, and that prepare for the correct airs of *Haute École*. Nevertheless, the riders whose horses execute the *passade* as it should be done can "be content with themselves and with their horses" and take their part of the praise that a master like Raabe awards to those who practice similar exercises well. I wish to all of you to merit that praise.

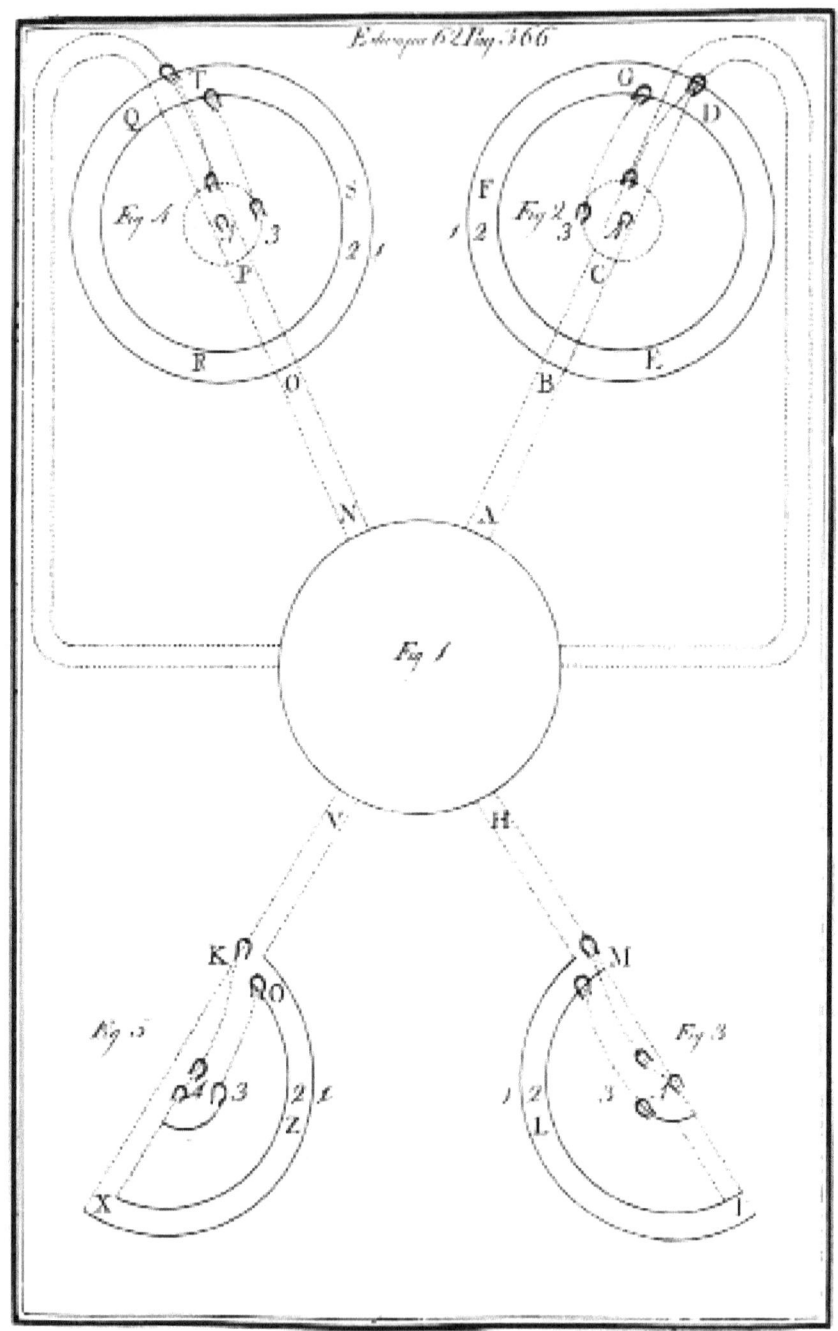

Pirouettes and demi-pirouettes

CHAPTER 3

CRITIQUE OF THE BAUCHERIST CONCEPT OF ACADEMIC HORSEMANSHIP

We hope that our study has begun to make clear our idea of true academic horsemanship. It remains for us to make a very clear outline of this horsemanship in order to distinguish it from the common practices that have moved away from it. In this last chapter, I will try to summarize my thoughts by showing that "The Art of Horsemanship and Dressage" is general, personal, and unique.

General, in that its principles are applicable to all horses with effective results.

Personal, because the details of implementation vary with the tact and sensitivity of each trainer.

Unique, since the goal to pursue is the same, whatever the means employed to achieve this.

THE PRINCIPLES APPLY TO EVERY HORSE

"The goal of the art is not only to ride a well-conformed animal, but also to take full advantage of those who were less well-gifted by nature." (Hünersdorf)

This sentence does not appear to find application in our day, where academic dressage addresses itself uniquely to horses of nearly perfect constitution. Therefore, it loses the character described by the German author.

It follows from this general concept, that an *écuyer* will be good if he succeeds in training a horse with excellent conformation, to make him execute the more difficult airs, but also if he is apt to train a horse of defective conformation, not in teaching him any particular air, but in at least balancing the three natural gaits.

Which of the two tasks is the more arduous? To explore the qualities of a good horse, or to transform a poorly constructed animal into a balanced mount?

Even if it is somewhat difficult to answer this question, I still want to emphasize that the passionate work necessary to make a good horse out of a bad one is rarely undertaken, because it requires a very pronounced taste for equestrian art, and above all, a knowledge and practice most rarely found today.

In the past, it was thought a good thing to train, and to render agreeable, all sorts of horses. Today, it seems that the taste for dressage is maintained mostly in those who have the means to buy horses that go well because they are the ones that win the tests.

And yet these are not the best horses for developing the rider's skill. It is not the amount of "tender pears" that perfects equestrian tact. And without sufficient tact, no dressage is possible. How many good horses are put to the side because they are badly ridden!

Baucher saw this very well. One can read in his *Méthode d'équitation basée sur de Nouveaux Principes* (6ᵉ éd., 1844, pp. 265, 266): "... But *écuyers* can pretend to results yet more brilliant. If they come to facilitate the good education of inferior horses, they popularize in the masses the study of horsemanship; they also put within reach of the purses of the middle class, so numerous in a country like ours which is based on equality, the practice of an art that until these days remained the privilege of those with great fortunes. All of my life, such was the goal of my work...."

The works of the masters often have the fault of applying only to horses of good conformation. It was in being conscious of the difficulty in correctly applying their excellent general principles that General Decarpentry, in his *Équitation Academic*, consecrated ninety pages of appendices to preparatory training in hand. There he examined the exceptions to the rule for numerous cases, and indicated the appropriate solutions.

**Composure.
Xerez ridden by Dom Diogo de Bragança.**

  The Art of Horsemanship must be suitable to be applied to every horse, and not only to those with excellent conformation, but to achieve that goal, we must admit exceptions to the rules, without departing from some absolute principles. How does one know what are the tolerable exceptions? It is through developing equestrian tact, listening to the advice of a master, by reading and constant practice.

  To bring a horse gifted with natural qualities to a stage of dressage that permits the rider to win a prize requires him to have a certain skill and to follow an effective method. But if he is to train a horse less favored by nature, only tact of an elevated degree will allow the resolution of difficulties.

**Hioral, trained and ridden by Professor Jaime Celestino da Costa.
"The perfect balance necessary to piaffe."
Colonel Challan-Belval.**

The two time winnner of Olympic Grand Prix Dressage, Commandant Reverony Saint-Cyr, declared, in an interview published in the Portuguese review *Diana*, that he did not make any use of flexions taught in hand. From this, one could conclude, if he had been well "judged," that the horse he rode had such a natural balance that he had no need of a gymnastic ordinarily considered fundamental to attain perfection in tests as difficult as those of academic dressage.

The horsemanship of today's "dressage" has become extremely mechanical, which is in contradiction with what General L'Hotte wrote: "No method, however logical and well organized it may be, will give infallible results, because any equestrian action to obtain the desired effect requires what no writing can provide: the appropriateness and the measure, in other words, the equestrian tact." (*Questions Équestres*,

Very collected canter, "...When the horse has flexible joints, a *tride* (lively, quick, short and ready) movement of the haunches, he will mark four beats... and show the correct cadence of a beautiful canter, that must be prompt in the haunches and collected in front..."
La Guérinière.

"Equestrian Questions" 1906, p. 190)

The extraordinary qualities of an *écuyer* required of Baucher to present the indomitable Géricault at the circus after four weeks of training would not be appreciated today by those who judge dressage tests. What would be the reason?

Today, the judges are influenced by flattering gaits, large gestures that only come from the horse's constitution and degree of blood, and nevertheless it is not perceived that, as M. Glahn said (article by Colonel Challan-Belval in *L'Éperon* of February 1957), "any exaggerated extension, any contraction, all that is not natural, proves that the manner of moving is impure, incorrect."

The current overall view of School horsemanship has become very restrained. It is limited to the presentation of horses of generally large size, regular conformation, ample gaits, and calm character.

It is truly necessary to be passionate for equestrian art to undertake the dressage of horses of hot temperament even if their conformation presents defects, and that is when, if the result achieved is good, that it is the most convincing.

The current form of dressage tests, with the programs known in advance, can only incite future competitors to repeat the same presentations. This leads them to the daily preoccupation to do what pleases the juries, without even saying to themselves that the judges' opinions could perhaps be erroneous, and, in any case, extremely questionable.

Are they sure that traditional *Haute École* is to be found in the official tests?

The competitors first seek to find horses that by their type will probably please the jury and that before all else will be sensible, if not to say dull. They have in mind the official equestrian shape that will give them a chance to place well.

They do not look to have a beautiful and vibrant horse, and to give him the training that is appropriate to him, but to choose a horse which they can require to present a test conforming to what the jury will likely find to its taste. This way, the official tests make for a "dressage" that becomes limited to a certain types of horses and takes away from the art the varied character that it should never have been forced to lose.

If the great "*écuyers*" had been given only one "template" into which they had to fit their mounts, they would have had many untrained horses left over. "For lack of development of his faculties, one finds only an ordinary mind where there was once a genius." (Baucher, *Passe-temps Équestres, Œuvres Complètes*, "Equestrian Pastimes, Complete Works" 13e éd., 1867, p. 240) Very few riders would be saddened by a situation of this type today. As soon as one of them has won a prize, he figures that he has achieved an equestrian result. This result only makes sense in comparison to the other contestants. It represents nothing in comparison to an art in which the horizon is vast. The rider is lacking in his role, which is to emphasize the natural qualities of his horse or to make up for the horse's faults.

It is quite evident that the rider will not compete, or in any case would not place, should he make out of an ugly horse, a beautiful one, out of a bad horse, a good one. This kind of achievement is the most interesting part of horsemanship. It requires maximum patience, observation, intelligence, and tact. Those are the rare qualities that a very few are willing to dedicate to an equestrian art that is tending to disappear.

According to the principle that the essential characteristic of academic dressage is the *rassembler*, the *écuyer*, deserving of the name, does not shrink from the difficult task of obtaining it from a horse that is not so naturally inclined, instead of limiting himself to riding those horses which are already gifted for it. One can understand how the masters of the XIX century gave the name "*équitation savante*" ("scholarly riding") to School horsemanship. With their study and practice they were brought to seek solutions to the problems of dressage, for which they had to call on knowledge derived from various sciences, physics, anatomy, psychology, etc. that completed equestrian science, properly said.

We have arrived at the sad conclusion that academic dressage has seen its flourishing period. The most extraordinary period was that of later Baucherism. Now, here we are in full regression with, as the Old School did, the use of only certain horses for lack of being able to modify the balance and temperament of the others.

Despite some elements of equestrian science derived from the results that, thanks to different instruments of measure, thanks to photography and later cinema, have been recorded with simplicity, clarity and method in books such as those of Doctor Le Bon, Commandant Chamorin, General Decarpentry, DVM André, despite the beauties and finer points of equestrian art that have been transmitted to us by the old *écuyers* who deigned to write – it is true that one must have the time to go find their works in the libraries and to be studious. In spite of the quality of the horses that the national and private studs continue to raise, one can not say that the riders of our era have kept up much interest in academic dressage. Most of them are content to practice horsemanship only as a sport. That is not bad in itself, far from it; but they have abandoned the art of the rider, the great ambition of whom should be to give his horse all the well-being and all of the brilliance possible. Those who are still interested in academic dressage are almost always only those "imitators of correctness" of whom La Guérinière spoke, and are more successful than those rarities who try to perpetuate the traditions of the masters. The latter are those that were appreciated by the Baron de Curnieu, learned hippologist. Here is what he said (cited by Wachter, *Aperçus Équestres*, "Equestrian Notes" 1862, p. 215), "The work in the *manège* is, for the *écuyer*, at once a study and a proof of his knowledge. ... A magnificent horse executing the elevated airs with nobility; a mediocre or defective horse, led to regular work; a formerly scared and dangerous horse, today calm and submissive, are as much for an *écuyer* certificates of glory and rights to public confidence. ... But an *écuyer* is only complete ... insofar as he can do on a horse all that is in the domain of equitation as it is largely understood ... and when he makes students like himself, good at everything."

METHODS ARE PERSONAL TO EACH *ÉCUYER*

"The horse is your mirror. He never flatters you. He reflects your temperament. He even reflects your vacillations. Never get angry with your horse, you might as well get angry with your mirror." (Binding, *Conseils poétiques à une Amazone bien-aimée*, "Poetical Advice to a Beloved *Amazone*"1949, French trans. Commandant E. Dupont.)

There have been many remarkable *écuyers*, many methods of horsemanship and dressage, but if someone asks us what is an infallible system of training, in conscience, we could not respond. Why? Because certain ways of acting are more appropriate to one rider than to another, furthermore it is necessary to adapt these ways to the horse that the rider is working. It is by the quality of his horses' work that a good *écuyer* is recognized. As long as the procedures employed to attain this quality do not cause any suffering on the part of the horse, the choice of these procedures becomes secondary.

In their lessons, *écuyers* put the accent on recommendations that were a refection of their personalities. "Sit, sit," repeated d'Abzac. Baucher's preoccupation was "Light, light" and M. de Vendeuil called out to his students, without a doubt already very skilled, "Brilliance, brilliance!"

Cesar Fiaschi accompanied the training of his horses with music. Fillis gave his horses impulsion at the girth, Raabe with the legs markedly to the rear, and contrary to most others, used the legs at the girth for the rein-back. The French School and the German School have

Mabrouck, trained and ridden by Captain Beudant, in a brilliant piaffe, in 1916."[...] The hind legs should not engage under the body too much, otherwise the movement is stopped by the shortening of the horse's base. (If they do so,) The line of the back lengthens and grows compared to the base of support, stability is compromised and the horse has difficulty finding a harmonious and steady balance. If on the contrary, the legs are straight, the horse finds it easier to change his balance in the vertical axis."
- Dressage regulations of the Federation Équestre Internationale, 1971.

brought their own contributions to dressage. Decarpentry did not find it a bad thing that they each kept their own character.

A great many horses have been very well trained in the pillars and with bits with enormous branches. Lateral horsemanship has been condemned in *Haute École* by certain *écuyers* (Fillis, Raabe), others were prone to it (Baucher in his Second Manner, L'Hotte, Faverot).

The genuine *écuyer* of today will outline the problems that he has to solve, help himself to special books, eventually ask for authoritative advice, and above all, call upon his equestrian tact.

We can usefully recall the opinion of General L'Hotte, expressed in the beginning of his *Questions Équestres* (Equestrian Questions 1906), "The means, used to the application of the principles, should not be fixed in an invariable way, whether it applies to the rider or to the horse."

If we add that he had wanted that above the door of every *manège*, one could read, "Reflect," we see by that confirmation that the art of horsemanship is personal in the methods to be employed, each horse having his own temperament and conformation. Each *écuyer* must choose the means applicable to each particular case, and in this choice, his equestrian education intervenes in a decisive manner. "Vary the means according to the nature of the horse," said Rousselet. (L'Hotte, *Un Officier de Cavalerie*, "A Cavalry Officer" 1905, p. 337.)

The personal side of horsemanship is reflected in the saying of the Arabs, that there are three things that they will never lend: wife, horse, and rifle. It is also evident in the desire expressed by General L'Hotte, that after his death, his three School horses would be put down; in Dumas' recommendation that one not work a horse in front of anyone else; in Baucher riding in the early morning hours before the arrival of his students, and in his writing about his sixteen new airs (*Œuvres Complètes*, (Complete Works) 13e éd., 1867, p. 377), "It is enough to say that their execution forms an equitation that becomes personal, that can only be the share of a studious man for whom it suffices to know that a thing is feasible for him to try it and bring it surely to a good result;" in the great Rousselet, not having reached an understanding with the horse, Capitaine, trained by Baucher, saying with a real modesty while getting off, "He is too fine for me."

So it was in the past; the assiduous *écuyer* came to find different procedures and new airs that gave a personal character to his equitation, instead of which today they follow the road that leads to a "standard rider," to a common method with all the conveniences and all the drawbacks that come from the repetition of the same model.

The consequence is a reduction in the number of airs that are being practiced, and we are not surprised to see some of them disappear from official tests. Faced with a certain shortage of contestants around the 1930s, there was even a question of doing away with the changes of lead at every stride, piaffe, and passage. To abolish the School airs is to limit the horse to that which he can do by himself, and not to be his master, giving him brilliance. I can see from here, some years into the atomic age, the astonishment and incredulity of a rider who will hear it said – because I could not believe that he would have gone so far as to read it – that Commandant Savary de Lancosme-Brèves, on 15 July 1856 travelled "in the presence of honorable persons" a kilometer at the trot to the rear in 5 minutes 25 seconds, a speed slightly higher than 10 km. per hour; that Beudant cantered in place while changing lead at every stride on his horse Turban; that Beudant obtained from his mare, Vallerine, pirouettes at the canter and even reversed pirouettes with the same changes of lead (*Souvenirs Équestres*, (Equestrian Memories) 1934, p.72); that he also did them at every stride in the canter to the rear on his horse Robersart (*Mains sans Jambes...*, (Hands without Legs....) 1945, pp. 110, 116): that he obtained from his horse Iris, on each lead, the canter on three legs forward and to the rear, the raised leg remaining completely extended (p. 123). Who would believe it?

A NOTE ON EXERCISES AND AIRS

In the "dressage" of today, it seems that riders forsake the School airs used as gymnastic exercises, executing them only when the horse does them by himself. It is an error to think that if the horse is not in condition enough to execute an air perfectly, better to not practice it. I think that there is no inconvenience in executing it despite the horse's deficiencies, since he is going to make progress, especially if the practice improves the horse's balance. An "open" passage might not be comparable to a correct passage, even so, its practice gymnasticizes the horse's back and legs and later the air will eventually approach a correct passage. The advantage to practicing certain airs as gymnastic exercises is increasing our interest in the training, at the same time as reducing the time that is normally necessary to its success.

I believe that in certain cases the airs can be envisioned as an efficacious means of training. The airs or figures of the *manège* constitute in themselves important exercises. It appears interesting to note the opinion of Wachter on this subject: "The Spanish Walk and the passage give to horses that up to then were of doubtful solidity, a rare precision in the movement of the legs." (*Aperçus Équestres*, (Equestrian Notes) 1862). One can read (pp. 151, 152): "For me, the experience proves that there is nothing quite so effective as these two airs, the Spanish walk and the passage, at re-establishing the regularity of all the other gaits, and at the same time making any bad disposition from an unruly attitude disappear. They make the horse extremely attentive. Excellent above all for young horses, whom these airs teach to march like young conscripts, they constitute a rational gymnastic that imparts strength, dexterity, mobility, solidity."

Montigny considered the passage not as an end, but as a means. Captain Raabe counseled teaching an air that he described (lift the forehand about $45°$ and balance on the hindquarters) as a *pesade* (and that he called, I know not why, a "courbette") as a preparation for the study of the pirouette.

In the end, what are exercises? They are the movements that the rider makes his horse execute so that their practice fortifies the joints and muscles and leads to balance.

What are the airs? They have been defined as "the stylization of the natural gaits." (Decarpentry) I would say for the comparison that I am making here that they are for me the "maximum expression of an exercise."

I mean to say by that statement that not only is the air the result of the best practice of the exercise, furthermore it must necessarily possess, when well done, the virtues of the corresponding exercise, elevated to their highest degree.

In the same way, for the School trot (exercise) raised to its maximum expression to become the passage (air), it must possess all the gymnastic qualities that the ordinary trot does not have. If the free canter (exercise) is to prepare for the School canter (air), it is the quality, existing or developed, in the first that is transmitted to second.

If we do not establish this rapport between the exercise and the corresponding air, horsemanship will no longer be a science and an art. Art that would only consist of the execution of the figures of the *manège,* would be separated from the science, that requires that exercises be practiced so that certain causes produce certain effects. If not, the airs would be no more than tours de force, in forced attitudes that have nothing to do with the natural gaits. Of course, a rigorous line of demarcation between exercise and air does not exist.

It can amount to a question of concept or fashion. For example, the piaffe that is today considered an air was also considered to be so by the Old School, but equally, it constituted an exercise preparatory to the elevated airs and the School jumps.

One can conclude that if it is normally fitting to begin with exercises to get to the airs, there will be cases where the direct practice of the air, when the horse will be disposed to produce it, will be most advantageous. Since the exercise executed at the highest level (air) leads to the quickest achievement of balance, and the training is improved as a result. For those who think, as we do, that good horsemanship is general, meaning it is applicable to all horses, this latter method of thinking is very important.

It was this idea that made Baucher, Raabe, and so many others begin by requiring, very early in the training, the piaffe in hand from the whip, before starting the study of it with the mounted horse.

Evidently, this dressage, in which the airs are none other than the greatest expression of the exercises, is within the reach of only a few riders. But just because we are not capable of putting it into practice does not mean that we must deny its utility. The interest that it presents and the relative rapidly of the results that it can produce are two of its most fascinating aspects. I am even convinced that to capture enthusiasts, it would be a good thing to make sufficiently advanced students ride already trained horses, and to help them to obtain some airs, more than to continue to make them practice monotonous exercises without progress, because today nobody has too much time to wait. It is only after having recognized the beauties of academic dressage that the youth inspired by them will have the desire to absorb the mysteries of academic dressage and the perseverance necessary to come by them.

Future School riders must also know that equestrian art is not limited to the use of qualities of a good horse, but rather that their field of experience extends to individuals that are physically and mentally much different. À propos of cadence, did not Baucher say in his *Passe-Temps Équestres* (1840) [Equestrian Pastimes]) , "The more that nature has been miserly, the more that art must be lavishly abundant."

Thus will be developed the personal side of horsemanship, because the "success" of training the defective horse comes nearly uniquely from tact, which will dictate to the rider not only the means to apply in each particular case, but also the modifications to introduce into the course of the method of training followed, in the face of the reactions of the horse that he is riding.

If, for example, the horse twists his poll in a lateral flexion of the neck, the normal placement of both hands must be modified, and it may be that it is necessary in some fashion for the hands to be used in the position in reverse of that habitually required, to wit, in the left lateral flexion, the left hand lower than the right hand. One of the greatest difficulties in dressage resides in the necessity of choosing the right means, whether they are carefully thought over or instantaneously decided. And this necessity is one of the elements of enchantment in which equestrian art can keep us.

THE GOAL OF DRESSAGE IS UNIQUE

What is the goal of Academic Equitation? It is balance in every gait and all the airs.

How to achieve the balance that Baucher called the primary genre? By the practice of lightness, taken in its largest and most profound sense, that is to say the use of minimum effort, as much on the part of the horse as that of the rider, for the production of the desired movement.

How does one appreciate this lightness?

By the more or less greater facility with which the rider can produce the descents of the hand and legs that allow the horse to go as if by himself continuing without the help of the aids, to execute whatever is asked of him.

Considering that the goal of horsemanship is unique, that is to know how to improve the horses' balance in order to ride them with ease, this ease requires obtaining their total lightness. Dressage must allow us to make the horse evolve with the minimum of effort and consequently with the maximum discretion in the aids.

If the patient and meticulous application of the various progressions proposed by the masters allows us to attack the problem of balance as a function of the sensitivity of each horse, and if it is up to each rider to choose and use the means that work the best on his horse, there is a unique goal to which the roads taken over the course of training must lead, and that is *obtaining the rassembler in total lightness.*

Never has this been quite so clearly expressed as by General Decarpentry in *L'Essential de la Méthode de Haute École de Raabe*,

"The Essential of the High School Method of Raabe." (1957)

After having emphasized that: "Relatively to his conformation and the placement of his strong and weak points, each subject can only give the full output of his mechanism in an attitude of the body that is proper to him..."

He summarizes, declaring, "The sole criteria to which the rider should gage his effort to obtain the 'full use' of the means of the horse is, as always, that of unchanging persistence in the lightness of his horse, submissive and willing, seeking instinctively, 'in the liberty on parole' of the *descent of the hand and legs*, the position that allows him to best satisfy his rider."

BIBLIOGRAPHY

ANDRADE (Fernando de Sommer d') *Toureio a Cavalo*, Lisbon, 1966

ANDRADE (Manoel Carlos de) *Luz da liberal e nobre Arte da Cavalleria*, Lisbon, 1760

Annee L'Hippique, Lausanne, 1959 – 1960; 1961 – 1962

Auto Hipico Portugues, Lisbon, 1954 – 1955; 1956 – 1957

BAUCHER (François) *Dictionnaire raisonné d'Équitation*, Paris, 1833;

----- *Méthode d'Équitation basée sur de nouveaux principes*, 6e éd., Paris, 1844, Jean- Michel Place, 1988;

See: François BAUCHER *A Method of Horsemanship Founded upon New Principles*, 9th French edition, 2nd American Edition, Philadelphia, 1852, reproduced by University of Michigan; also Hardpress;

See: Hilda NELSON *François Baucher, The Man and his Method*, Xenophon Press 2012;

----- *Œuvres Complètes, Méthode d'Équitation basée sur de nouveaux principes*, 12e éd., Paris, 1864, Jean-Michel Place, 1988;

----- *Œuvres Complètes, Méthode d'Équitation basée sur de nouveaux principes*, 13e éd., Paris, 1867, Jean-Michel Pace, 1988;

----- *Méthode d'Équitation*, 14ᵉ éd., Paris, 1874, Jean-Michel Place, 1988

Captain Étienne BEUDANT, *Dressage du Cheval de Selle*, 1ʳᵉ éd., Paris, 1929;

----- *Souvenirs Équestres*, Paris, 1934;

----- *Mains sans jambs* [...], Lyon, 1945;

----- *Dressage du Cheval de Selle*, 3ᵉ éd., Paris, 1948

Rudolf G. BINDING *Conseils poétique à une Amazone bien-aimée*, trans. by Commandant Edouard Dupont, Paris, 1949

Boletim pecuario, Lisbon, 1943

Conde de BORNOS *Reglas de Torear*, 1644

Commandant Isidore DAUDEL *Méthode d'Équitation et de Dressage*, Paris, 1857

General Albert DECARPENTRY *Piaffer et Passage*, Paris, PSR, 2000;

 See: *Piaffe and Passage*, Xenophon Press 2012;

----- *Baucher et son École*, Paris, 1948, Jean-Michel Place, 1990;

See: *Baucher and his School*, Xenophon Press, Virginia 2011

----- *Équitation Academique*, Paris, 1949, Lavauzelle, 1991;

 See: *Academic Equitation*, trans. by Nicole Bartle, J. A. Allen, London, 1971; Trafalgar Square, Classic Edition, North Pomfret, 2001;

----- *Les Maîtres Écuyers du Manège de Saumur*, Paris, 1954, Lavauzelle, 1991;

----- *L'Essential de la Méthode de Haute École de Raabe*, Paris, 1957

DUARTE, King of Portugal *Livro da ensinança de bem cavalgar toda sela*, 1438

See: *The Royal Book of Jousting, Horsemanship and Knightly Combat, A Translation into English of King Dom Duarte's 1438 Treatise: Livro da ensinança de bem cavalgar toda sela*, "The Art of Riding in Every Saddle," Trans. by Antonio Franco Preto; The Chivalry Bookshelf

Marquis Jean-François DUCROC DE CHABANNES *Cours élémentaire et analytique d'Équitation au résumé des principes de M. d'Auvergne*, Paris, 1827

Charles-Louis Mercier DUPATY DE CLAM *Practique de l'Équitation*, Paris,

1769;

----- *La Science & l'Art de l'Équitation*, Paris, 1776

L'Éperon, Paris, Feb. 1956, Feb. 1957, Jun. 1965

General François FAVEROT DE KERBRECH *Dressage Méthodique du Cheval de Selle d'après les derniers enseignments de F. Baucher*, recueillis par un de ses élèves, Paris, 1891;

See: FAVEROT DE KERBRECH *Methodical Dressage of the Riding Horse* and *Dressage of the Outdoor Horse,* Xenophon Press, 2010

Antonio GALVÃO DE ANDRADE *Arte de Cavallaria de Gineta...,* Lisbon, 1678

Maxime GAUSSEN *Étude sur l'Équitation Savante*, Paris, 1893

Commandant Adolphe GERHARDT *Manuel d'Equitation*, Paris, 1859;

----- *La Verité sur la Méthode Baucher ancienne et nouvelle*, Paris, 1869

Captain Alexandre GUÉRIN *École du Calvalier au Manège*, Saumur, 1851;

----- *Dressage du Cheval de Guerre*, Saumur, 1860

George GUILLET *Le Dictionnaire du Gentilhomme*, Paris, 1678

Louis HÜNERSDORF *Équitation Allemande, méthode la plus facile et la plus naturelle pour dresser le Cheval d'Officier et d'Amateur*, 1791 (trans. From 6th ed., 1840, by Captain Armand de Brochowsky, Brussels, 1843

François Robichon de LA GUÉRINIÈRE *École de Cavalerie*, éd. In-octavo, Paris, 1754

See: *École de Cavalerie Part Two*, Xenophon Press, 1992;

General Alexis L'HOTTE *Un Officier de Cavalerie*, 1905;

----- *Question Équestres*, Paris, 1906;

See: Hilda NELSON *Alexis François L'Hotte, The Quest for Lightness in Equitation*, J. A. Allen, London, 1997

Commandant Jean LICART *L'Équitation raisonnée*, 1re éd., Bordeaux, 1943;

----- *Évolutions Équestres à travers les ages*, Olivier Perrin Éditeur, Paris, 1963

Christoff Jacob LIEBENS *Reitbuch*, Leipzig, 1665

François MUSANY *Propos d'un Écuyer*, Paris, 1895

Nuno OLIVEIRA *Œuvres Complètes*, Paris, 2006

Jules PELLIER (fils) *L'Équitation practique*, 3ᵉ éd., 1875

Antonio PEREYRA REGO *Instrução da Cavallaria de Brida [...],* Coïmbra, 1679

Antoine de PLUVINEL *L'Instruction de Roy en l'exercise de Monter à Cheval*, Paris, 1625; See: *The Maneige Royal*, Xenophon Press 2010

Colonel Alois PODHAJSKY *Die Spanische Hofreitschule*, Vienna, 1948;

----- *L'Équitation* (Trans. from German by Commandant Édouard Dupont), Paris, 1968

Captain Charles RAABE *Examen du bauchérism réduit à sa plus simple expression*, M. Rul, Paris, 1857;

----- *Méthode de Haute École d'Équitation*, Marseilles, 1863

Règlement sur les Exercices de la Cavalerie, Paris, 1876

Règlement des Concours de Dressage de la Fédération Équestre Internationale,

10ᵉ éd., Brussels, 1958

13ᵉ éd., Brussels, 1971

Louis RUL *Le baucherism réduit à sa plus simple expression*, Paris, 1857

Captain Jacques de SAINTE-PHALLE *Équitation*, Paris, 1907

SIND (Baron de) *L'Art du Manége*, 3ᵉ éd., Vienna, 1774

Baron de VAUX *Écuyers et Écuyères*, Paris, 1893

Lieutenant Louis WACHTER , *Aperçus Équestres*, Paris, 1862

CREDITS

All the schooling diagrams are extracted from the work of Manoel Carlos de Andrade, *Luz da liberal e nobre Arte da Cavallaria,* Lisbon, 1790.
All of the photographs come from the private collections of Diogo de Bragança and René Bacharach.

Xenophon Press Library

Xenophon Press continues to bring new works to print in the English language whether they be new works, such as this one, or translations of older works. Xenophon Press is dedicated to the preservation of classical equestrian literature.

Available at www.XenophonPress.com

30 Years with Master Nuno Oliveira, Michel Henriquet 2011

A Rider's Survival from Tyranny, Charles de Kunffy 2012

Another Horsemanship, Jean-Claude Racinet, 1994

Art of the Lusitano, Yglesias de Oliveira, 2012

Baucher and His School, General Decarpentry 2011

Dressage in the French Tradition, Dom Diogo de Bragança 2011

École de *Cavalerie Part II,* François Robichon de la Guérinière 1992

Equine Osteopathy: What the Horses Have Told Me, Giniaux 2014

François Baucher: The Man and His Method, Baucher/Nelson, 2013

Great Horsewomen of the 19th Century in the Circus, Nelson 2015

Gymnastic Exercises for Horses Volume II, Eleanor Russell 2013

H. Dv. 12 Cavalry Manual of Horsemanship, Reinhold 2014

Healing Hands, Dominique Giniaux, DVM 1998

Horse Training: Outdoors and High School, Etienne Beudant 2014

Legacy of Master Nuno Oliveira, Stephanie Millham 2013

Methodical Dressage of the Riding Horse, Faverot de Kerbrech 2010

Racinet Explains Baucher, Jean-Claude Racinet 1997

The Art of Traditional Dressage, Volume I DVD, de Kunffy 2013

The Ethics and Passions of Dressage Expanded Ed., de Kunffy 2013

The Gymnasium of the Horse, Gustav Steinbrecht 2011

The Italian Tradition of Equestrian Art, Tomassini 2014

The Maneige Royal, Antoine de Pluvinel 2010

The Portuguese School of Equestrian Art, de Oliveira/da Costa, 2012

The Science and Art of Riding with Lightness, Stodulka 2014

The Spanish Riding School & Piaffe and Passage, Decarpentry 2013

Total Horsemanship, Jean-Claude Racinet 1999

Wisdom of Master Nuno Oliveira, Antoine de Coux 2012

www.ingramcontent.com/pod-product-compliance
Lightning Source LLC
Chambersburg PA
CBHW050634300426
44112CB00012B/1795